PUBLIC SPEAKING FOR MINISTERS

PUBLIC SPEAKING FOR MINISTERS

BY

ARTHUR STEVENS PHELPS

Revised by
LESTER R. DE KOSTER

BAKER BOOK HOUSE
Grand Rapids, Michigan

Previously published
under the title
Speaking in Public

ISBN: 0-8010-6894-0

Revised Edition
First printing, April 1964
Second printing, December 1967
Third printing, September 1969
Fourth printing, September 1971
Fifth printing, January 1974
Sixth printing, July 1976

Library of Congress Catalog Card Number: 58-8388

Copyright, 1958, by

BAKER BOOK HOUSE

PHOTOLITHOPRINTED BY CUSHING - MALLOY, INC.
ANN ARBOR, MICHIGAN, UNITED STATES OF AMERICA

PREFACE

The study of the "art of all arts," as Henry Clay called speaking in public, is no longer limited to the curricula of schools and colleges. Thousands of business and professional men, without unusual speaking talent, want to learn how to acquit themselves creditably before an audience. "How can I overcome stage fright?" "How should I prepare and deliver a popular after-dinner talk?" "Can I be armed to meet unexpected situations?" "How can a young minister, lawyer, or dramatist win out with an audience?" It is to meet such questions as these in a sympathetic and understanding way that these lectures are published. There are a host of terrifying problems faced by every speaker in pulpit and platform that the conventional books on the subject have overlooked, and most professors of homiletics and "oratory" have passed by. In my course as a student, professors in this department seemed to have forgotten that there are audiences; and the "holy tone" (one of the deadliest obstacles to usefulness), mannerisms, illustrations, after-dinner speaking, lecturing, were never mentioned, and indeed a thousand other things that every speaker must face—after he gets on the platform—left for him to guess at. And as for being interesting, bridging the chasm that yawns between desk and benches, the discussion of such a thing is too often felt by the profession to lower its standards of dignity.

To assist those preparing for the ministry, as well as to stimulate those already in it, to bridge more effectively that gap between pulpit and pew is the aim of the following chapters. It is the hope of the author that they may also be of assistance to the growing number of laymen who in church groups, in business or political or union meetings, or in various other ways and places dedicate themselves to bringing truth and light to their fellows by way of public speech.

CONTENTS

1

IMPORTANCE OF EFFECTIVE
PUBLIC SPEAKING

The ability to speak effectively in public is now a matter of importance to almost every calling. There come times to all of us when, like John Alden, we must speak for ourselves. Great causes need defenders. To stand before an expectant audience, or before an expectant individual, with nothing to say or, which is as unfortunate, with much to say and without the ability to say it, is one of the most embarrassing situations in life.

The majority of public addresses are failures. Jean Francois Millet said: "I think things had better not be said at all, than said weakly." How many addresses have you heard during the past six months that have held your interest, stirred your feelings, or roused your will? And if they have not accomplished one or all three of these things, they have to a degree done the opposite. Dullness is eloquent—for the opposite side. A school teacher and a preacher are as much in duty bound to be interesting as a popular lecturer. The more important a subject is, the more reason for giving it carrying power. An editorial writer in one of the most widely circulated students' dailies in the country recently asked:

> "When a price is set on undergraduate cleverness and a penalty placed on triteness, why is it considered proper by those who sit in the hallowed halls of authority, that of all those of whom originality should be exacted, professors alone are exempt?
>
> "The dry-as-dust lecturer is subject to no penalties. He is on hand at all times, smugly basking in the sunlight of his own platitudes, unctuously clearing his throat by way of puncturing his remarks, blissfully unaware of the hatred brooding in the breasts of his unwilling audience."

Speaking in public is the most difficult of all the arts, perhaps because it is the most valuable. It is the most difficult of the arts, too, because there are so many chances to fail. Cicero lamented: "There is nothing more rare among men than a perfect orator." In his *De Oratore:* "There is requisite to the orator the acuteness of the logician, the subtlety of the philosopher, the skilful harmony, almost, of the poet, the memory of a lawyer, the tragedian's voice, and the gesticulation of the most finished actors."

Animated actors are often dull speakers. Some eminent literary men are almost as famous for their failures on the platform as for their successes with the pen. Witness Rousseau, Julian Hawthorne, Lamennais, Goldsmith who "wrote like an angel, and talked like poor Poll." Harold Bell Wright, who has reaped a fortune from his books, received, it is said, almost a starvation salary for his preaching. Perhaps it was he who tells of the colored exhorter who, after telling an acquaintance that he got only fifty dollars as a year's salary, and receiving the sympathetic response: "It is a disgrace to the church to pay you such a small salary!" answered: "Ah don't know, boss, did yo' evah hear me preach?" The arts of saying and writing things, the same things, are different arts.

Charming and inspiring conversationalists are sometimes worse than dumb before an audience. Both speakers and talkers have the gift of speech, but each is proverbially lacking in the other's art. They differ more widely than chamber-music and the oratorio. It is strange that the addition or subtraction of a certain number of hearers changes the art of vocal expression to a foreign field! Who would want to hear on the platform Socrates or Dr. Samuel Johnson, the world's two most famous conversationalists?

Unfortunately, the majority of men that have chosen speaking in public as their profession are pitiably poor speakers. Many ministers are failures in the pulpit. The sheep do not want to hear their voice. Their auditors bring to church more religious zeal than they carry away. If it were not for the rich content of the gospel which they preach, they would not be worth listening to. It is sad that a hearer has to force himself to listen to what should be the breath of heaven to him; and that the good seed finds its chief impediment in the sower. "Of the three places," writes Thomas Embley Osmun, "where we hear most public speaking and reading—our courts of law, our theatres, and our churches—the place where we hear the best elocution is the first, and the place where we hear the worst elocution is the last." An eloquent young preacher came to the study of the Reverend F. F. Emerson, a thoughtful, but dull speaker, and said to him: "If I had your sermons, or you my delivery, we could carry all before us!" During Mr. Emerson's next summer vacation, some one broke into his house and stole his sermons. I am not offering this incident as a solution of the difficulty.

We frequently hear it said that speaking in public has had its day: with the host of high class periodicals and books that are flooding the press, we do not need the platform any longer. The objection is shallow. Good speaking has many elements of superiority over good books. It makes thought alive; its impression goes deeper; its meaning is clearer through the concrete medium of gesticulation; the speaker's personal magnetism is a vital influence; and warmth of social feeling is to be found only in a congregation of one's fellows. I once heard the outline of a series of addresses on *The Fallacy of Well Known Proverbs*. Perhaps the most absurd of such trite proverbs is: "Talk is cheap." No talk could well be cheaper than that saying.

Talk is the mightiest force in the world. That way lies education. Not only does talk teach others; it teaches the talker most of all. An idea is never really our own until we have imparted it to another. To keep an idea give it away. The Declaration of Independence is talk. The speech of Lincoln at the battlefield of Gettysburg, despite his modest declaration to the contrary, has become more famous than the battle itself. Talk has made the reputation of the Tower of Babel. Talk has made the financial success of the telephone, the phonograph, the radio. The Sermon on the Mount was talk. So were the Ten Commandments—though in that case actions speak louder than words. What is a marriage proposal but talk? If "talk is cheap," how explain the influence of propaganda? Abraham Lincoln, striking off the iron shackles of slavery, replaced them with the golden fetters of public opinion: "Public sentiment is everything: with public sentiment, nothing can fail; without it, nothing can succeed. Consequently he who moulds public sentiment goes deeper than he who enacts statutes or pronounces decisions. He makes

statutes and decisions possible or impossible to be executed."
When John the mystic evangelist sought a metaphor with which
to describe the relation that the Messiah bore to the Father, he
called Him the *Word* of God. A luminous phrase! A word is
the expression of the inner life. Through words, as across a
bridge, heart travels to heart.

Today, when books and periodical literature have an unprece-
dentedly wide circulation, oratory has sprung into a place of
prominence that it has never known before. Every book and
lecture on business efficiency gives speakability prime emphasis.
Shelf after shelf in the public library is devoted to it. It holds an
increasingly conspicuous place in the curricula of colleges and
schools. Advertisements in the papers announce extension
courses and night schools where business clerks and members of
social clubs shall have opportunity for the study and practice of
this the highest of the arts. It is even being taught by mail.

It is often said that the pulpit is the minister's throne. While
executive management and pastoral work are of vital importance,
yet every school of theology places preaching ability as supreme
among ministerial gifts. Churches are looking for preaching
pastors. Candidates for the pastorate are not asked to set up a
sample organization, but to preach sample sermons, much as one
may regret this unfair and disproportionate method of rating
ability. So difficult to find are arresting and convincing speakers,
that our great city churches frequently call to their pulpits men
of other denominational affiliations, and employ assistants to
take charge of administration and pastoral service. More and
more, even if several churches have to combine to bring it about,
are congregations coming to see that men of special gifts should
be kept free to exercise them, unhampered by details that associates can perform.

Forty years ago, not only was debating not taught in the class-
room, but there were no intercollegiate debates, no school or
college debating societies. Public forums were unknown. The
lawyer had to learn in the law school to defend a case; others had
to depend on their native talent for repartee in an emergency.
The Oxford Union in England has shown American students
the value of the public debate. For, in a very real sense, every
public utterance is a debate, the fact that the opponents in the

audience have no chance to "come back" making them the more dangerous, and difficult to convince. That is why Henry Ward Beecher encouraged his church members to express opposition in his prayer-meetings.

The high place of public speech in our day is proved also by the extraordinary fame of great masters on the platform. When Moody and Sankey proposed to hire the circus tent for evangelistic services, the circus proprietors laughed at them. But the vast throngs swelling in and looking for seats told its own story. I have seen police compelled to club the crowds that threatened to wreck the opening passageways by their furious zeal to get in. At the services of Billy Sunday, auditors climbed up among the rafters, at risk of life and limb, to hear him speak. Evangelist Billy Graham filled Madison Square Garden night after night for weeks on end, and his words drew men and women irresistibly forward. The late Mr. Bryan and others have had similar experiences. Political opponents who came to hiss have ended by throwing their hats in the air, howling approval of sentiments that they knew they did not believe. This Commoner, who had formed the habit of running in vain for the presidency, dominated the views of his party as soon as he rose to speak.

The key to success on the platform will not be found in the pockets of the punctilious observer of set rules for speaking in public. Of course, for the serious student of speech such knowledge is important background, but in trying to remember them, we should fail to observe them. The very effort is distracting from the purpose in view. I attended a lecture of the professor of public speaking at a well-known Boston theological seminary. He had drawn on the blackboard a scientific diagram of the human throat, showing the physiographic location of the organs of speech. Suppose that while you were delivering an address to a thousand high school students on *Fair Play,* you were to be asking yourself: "Did that tone come from my trachea, aesophagus, or diaphragm?" where, oh where, would you find your audience when you came to? It is of importance to study the proper use and register of your voice as the medium of expression, as we shall do, later; but the process of steel-making does not interest the surgeon as he uses the knife. The rules of speaking, like those of all the arts, must be so assiduously practiced in private that they become the unconscious guides of public performance.

Speaking is self-expression. It is not a mere figure of speech to say that a speaker "expresses himself" well or ill. When we hear that this and that was said, we ask at once: "Who said it?" Was it the man behind the gun, or the man behind the tree? It is for this reason that the student of public speech lays his emphasis on the speaker, the *self* that lies back of all that is to be spoken. The less a man knows, the more he talks and the less he says. "The cannon must be larger than the shot it puts." That is why a familiar thought when spoken by a strong man is given new meaning. It is stamped with his personality. Almost anything is striking, if uttered by the right lips. While engaged in mission work when I was in the Divinity School, a woman on whom I called said she had often thought of what her pastor had said. "What was it?" I asked. "He said: 'This is a busy world.' " The good seed had evidently not fallen on stony ground. But as a fact, though the world is too old for original thoughts, every thought strained through an original mind becomes original. Such original thoughts, uttered in deep earnest and under the discipline of study and practice, kindle response and action in those who hear them. The seeming ease of the artist is the hard won result of long practice.

While there is a wide variety of speeches to which the gift of speaking in public is put, yet the laws of the game, the principles that make for success or failure, are similar. That is why books and courses of study in this field have so live an appeal. I have intimated that every speech is a contest between the speaker and his audience. When he mounts the pulpit or the soap-box, he throws down the gauntlet. There may be no consciousness of competition on either side, but it is there. As in the case of an auctioneer and the buyers, so in every assembly either the rostrum or the benches will get the victory. The result is like that of the baseball series: one day the "Yankees" win, the next day the "Indians." The speaker has warmed the cold, instructed the ignorant, saved the sinner, halted the speeder, interested the stupid; or else he has slunk from his elevation in defeat with the consciousness that the load was too heavy for him to lift. Is there any humiliation on earth equal to that of sneaking, like a whipped cur, from the arena of public speech, feeling that the loftiest, purest efforts of your life have been thrown back in your face? "Is there any hell," cried poor Keats, "fiercer than the failure in a great object?" Is there on the earth any exaltation of spirit equal to that of having "swept the boards"? Whether in thunders of applause, or in the silence of tear-stained faces, the winner in this contest has won such a reward as few situations have the wealth to offer.

Manifold as are the causes of defeat to a speaker, as many are the reasons for success in his calling. He must speak well, first, to pay the debt he owes his audience. A public office is a public trust. Every calling is a mortgage held by the public. St. Paul, entering upon his calling, acknowledges: "I am a debtor, both to Greeks and to barbarians; as far as in me lies, I am a debtor." In taking the platform, you have acknowledged your debt. Expectant faces must not be disappointed.

You must speak well, to uphold the reputation of your profession. The chief argument for or against any occupation is the men that occupy themselves with it. Success is contagious: and every man that succeeds is a living invitation to choose his way of life. How many telephone operators Alexander Graham Bell made! How many aviators Charles Lindbergh! In Webster's court room every one wanted to be a lawyer; in Beecher's congregation a minister. Who but pulpiteers are to be blamed for the phrase, "dry as preaching"? When a man wants to give stimulating advice to a friend, why does he begin by saying: "Now, I'm not going to preach to you"? He ought to wish he could. Why does the cinema sometimes make the Protestant minister ridiculous? It is because some ministers whom the scenario artist has heard made their profession ridiculous. When a speaker addresses an audience who are accustomed to listening to a platform king, he has their attention from the start: and when he follows "a mere discharger of words," he must fight for attention in every word he speaks. His congregations are right: how else can they judge of a profession than by its representatives? By thy words thou shalt be justified, and by thy words thou shalt be condemned. Commend your calling by your practice.

Your future depends on your success. You must earn your

salary, or lose it. The same thing is true of your reputation. To speak well, is to win invitations to speak; and each invitation accepted increases the ability to speak well. Dividends at interest pay dividends: to him that hath shall be given.

Speaking well has cultural value for the speaker. Senator Beveridge, after defining oratory as one of the fine arts, adds: "Art is the highest function of the mind and soul of man." To appreciate art to the full, one must become an artist. The alert pursuit of a high vocation lifts every faculty of the mind. Everything that one does well brings self-criticism of everything else one is doing. "The better is the enemy of the best." On many a grave, if the truth were told, would be found written the epitaph: "Too easily satisfied." Every one can do better than he thinks. There is a sleeping giant within that needs only the noise of serviceable industry to awaken it. There are men of force on the platform today who, when they began, had everything against them: a thin voice, clumsy mannerisms, and a hangdog spirit.

To defend exalted themes in resistless speech, is to hold human history in your hands. Divinity students laughed at one of their classmates who refused to accept any recreational invitation for the afternoon before he was to preach: "The destiny of men may hang on that address," he declared. His great New York pastorate proved him right. The listener's life is what the speaker makes it. "Life and death are in the power of the tongue." When Rockefeller was brought forward for church membership as a boy, it is said, a prominent church official objected: "Well, I suppose there is no harm in letting such children come into the church, if they want to; but of course they can be of no financial value." The speaker draws his bow at a venture: how little he knows the mark he hits! There were two hundred additions to a church from a series of services. A similar series was held contemporaneously elsewhere, with only one convert. The names of the two hundred have all been forgotten. The single convert was David Livingstone. Earnest speech is gifted with parenthood. The late Sylvester Horne boldly declared: "The appearance of a true preacher is the greatest gift that any nation can have." He points the path to character.

The truth is on trial, and we are the witnesses. What verdict will the jury render?

2

PLACE OF PUBLIC SPEAKING
IN MODERN LIFE

The higher the speaker values his work, the more personal interest he will take in it; and the more interest he takes in it, the greater the likelihood of his making good. If we like a job, we will work at it.

The speaker's art is complementary to that of the administrator. Reason and emotion do not occupy two separate compartments of the brain, as Benedetto Croce, the Italian philosopher, has pointed out; they are both activities of the same mind. Though speech belongs to the emotional temperament, yet the speaker uses the executive temper in every address. And every executive makes addresses to his employees. Yet, rare is the individual that possesses both of these faculties in a marked degree. As far as our observation of men goes, the speaking function and the executive function appear to be mutually exclusive. Where one leaves off, the other begins. General U. S. Grant, one of the most famous of executives, was proverbially silent; while William Jennings Bryan, one of the most eloquent of speakers, resigned from the Cabinet of counsellors. The Church of the future must have at least two heads, an executive head in whose hands shall rest the administration of the thousand and one activities of the modern parish, and an inspirational head who shall exercise the yet rarer platform gifts. Every great commercial institution recognizes this dualism. The reader of the Bible can easily distinguish between the writings of the priest and the prophet, and in general literature, between an essay and an oration.

The art of oratory differs also from that of elocution. Elocution is reciting that which has been written by another; oratory is speaking one's own matter. A writer has said that elocution is child's play, and public speaking a man's work. But elocution, though an inferior art, is a valuable handmaid to oratory. Every student should be trained in the work of interpreting the thought, and entering into the emotion of the world's great speakers. There is inspiration in them which at first he cannot find in his own gropings. A course in elocution will also teach him how to read aloud—a thing that old-fashioned oratory failed to do. The parrot-reading of Scriptures and hymns in the average church service is a disgrace to the ministry. Small wonder these features have come in public esteem to be relegated from their proper place of worship by the patronizing term "opening exercises"! Why should a preacher complain of his people coming in late to service, when his whole attitude seems to say: "We will hurry this stuff out of the way, and then you will get a chance to hear *me*"? These exercises form a vital part of public utterance, and are sometimes the only vital thing the audience finds to carry away.

That the place of public speech in modern life is a place of preeminent consequence, is recognized. Language was spoken before it was written, the very word *language* being derived from the Latin *lingua,* tongue. The great sums expended for municipal auditoriums and for church buildings attest the prime place of speaking in public. The business man depends on publicity for the sale of his goods. The office extends its tentacles through the tongue of its commercial travelers. The various departments of the church are vitalized, and its members won, by the pulpit. It is by speech that the attorney defends our peace and possessions; the physician our health; the promoter seeks our wealth; the humorist provides our entertainment; the teacher our education; the lecturer our instruction; the politician runs our government; the preacher reforms our character.

Its importance is not lessened by the difficulty of success. Value costs. The speaker in public finds new heights to climb as he ascends. The work of his art is a lifelong study. In every speech, he makes discoveries. There is something always to learn, and having learned to bear in mind. Many books on public speaking declare that it is impossible to fasten one's mind on the principles of speaking and on one's speech at the same time. While the rules carefully practiced in private may largely be forgotten during public speech, and should be also; none-the-less, the speaker must in some sense observe the effectiveness of his own techniques during actual speaking. Will this gesture do? Is this phrase provocative of response? Is this joke worth trying again? Is the speech too long? Should I move about more? or less? Are my sentences too long? Are they too involved? Am I talking over the heads of some, or too simply for others? Such questions must also come to the mind even as the speech is being delivered. But let the posture, the voice, the gesture, the facial expression have been so thought upon, so worked out at home that in the moment of speaking they may be employed without conscious attention. For while the mind would be hampered, in the heat of addressing an audience, by trying to remember countless rules, the necessary rules may be written down privately, as learned from books, or picked up by experience, and then thought over constantly and practiced until they become natural and spontaneous. Easy as it looks to an outsider, the ability to interest and uplift an audience is purchased at almost infinite cost of application and labor. In certain respects preaching is more difficult than other kinds of speaking. The same audience faces the preacher every time he goes into the pulpit; he must preach at set hours, and not only when he feels like it, and there are occasions when the sound of a church bell makes him want to take to the woods; he lacks the inspiration of the "special occasion"; he is confined to a limited range of themes; he has to speak constantly, his regular appointments averaging from thrice a week up; many ministers average more than one address daily for weeks at a time; most of his hearers are already convinced of the truth of what he is to say; and his audience know that he is *paid* to talk. Therefore, he should make the more assiduous effort to succeed. If the greater number fail in this difficult art, there is at least the more room for the survivors. The gale that blows out a small fire makes a serious one burn the hotter. The waters that drowned the world lifted Noah.

Of so great value is this speaking art, that every one ambitious to win should be encouraged. The more important, the more worth while the pains necessary to its study. There is a false notion abroad that if you *study* public speaking, it will make you artificial. There never was more arrant nonsense than the notion that all that is necessary is to "pull out the bung and let nature caper." No one is so quick as Dame Nature to resent and punish such insults. Would you like a garage hand to depend on "the inspiration of the moment" for his ability to repair your car? Training aids instinct. Emerson advises us that "a certain mechanical perfection must precede every art." The more difficult the art, the more thorough the training must be. The manner of delivery is as important to a speaker as it is to a baseball pitcher. While we would modify the famous saying of Quintilian that "orators are made, poets born," by acknowledging that the best orators are born with eloquent tongues, yet even the born speaker is made better by study. Genius is born, success earned. Some are born speakers, and success is as natural to them as breathing. Those that are not so fortunate can never hope to compete with them as equals, nor to make a flaming success on the platform. But by diligent study and unremitting toil, they can be assured of becoming convincing and acceptable speakers. Hard working mediocrity stands a better chance in the long run than lazy genius.

Even after the best speech, the effect is hardly a hundreth part of the effort expended, though there are exceptional occasions when an address has changed the course of human history and set a nation on fire. The young speaker should improve every opportunity to practice, not only accepting all invitations that come his way, but taking voluntary part in public gatherings for political, religious or other ends, where he may render real service. It was speaking in the country caucus that made Lincoln president. You learn to express yourself by expression; to feel by feeling; to think by thinking. The best books on speaking have been written by good speakers; the student should become familiar with them. He should make it a point to hear great speakers, and take notes of what he considers their good and their bad points. Spurgeon said he disliked to hear the average preacher, for he was thinking how much better he could do it himself. Such inner comparisons are worth while, as is also the practice of talking over the principles of apposite speech with other students and, as opportunity affords, with great preachers and other orators. The student's reading should include the biographies of famous orators past and present, as well as a careful study of great orations and sermons. You can learn more from great speakers than from books.

Because the ability to speak effectively is so difficult, success brings the greater triumph. The speaker succeeds when he least expects it. It is a singular fact that he is frequently astray in his own judgments in this matter. An audience will hail such victories with delight. Nothing in the way of praise, response, or admiration is too good to give the eloquent speaker. His career is like that of a conquering hero in war time. The crowds that gather, an hour before the time, the air of expectancy, the thrill that his power over them brings to him, the reflection afterwards, kindle a joy that little else on earth can equal. Success also brings humility, as if he were only a spectator at a scene in which another above and, as it were, outside of himself had been the real actor. His only enemy in the hour of triumph is the envious aspirant for popular applause who has witnessed his superior's exaltation. It is characteristic of small minds not to learn from the self-denial and methods by which another advances in his calling, but to decry them as of little worth; to be angry at the success of another, instead of seeking the remedy for their own failure. One wishes that a rejoinder were at hand like that of the friend whose comrade at the time of the French Revolution proposed to start a new religion: "What method would you use?" asked the enthusiast. To which the reply: "I should advise you to get yourself crucified, and on the third day rise from the dead: that worked well the other time." Cynicism is a smoke-screen. Those that are great of heart take delight in the greatness of another. Hume, the skeptic, "went great distances to hear doctrines [from Whitefield] that he detested, delivered in a style that fascinated him."

The place of public speech in behalf of a momentous cause is emphasized by public need. To serve the neediest first, is true patriotism. I asked a young man who was making an excellent living as a mechanic why he had decided to leave his work for the ministry. His face grew thoughtful in his reply: "Because the need is so great." It was not rewards of popular speech that he sought, but its value to the common weal. A true man aims

not at eloquence, but at effectiveness. A whole course of lectures
on Speaking in Public are summed up in the words:

MAKE IT YOUR AIM NOT TO DO WELL, BUT TO DO GOOD.

The defender of truths on which the history of the race hangs,
may well be proud of his work. Great men stand in awe of their
calling. Painters have arrayed themselves in princely raiment,
clergymen in satin robes, military generals wear gorgeous uni-
forms, to show the exalted worth of what they do.

The place of public speech is a place of adaption to all phases
of life. How varied the interests of men! The old advice has it,
"To each a word in due season." The same sentence may rebuke,
encourage, cheer, rouse, console, inspire. A speech is not like a
rifle bullet, aimed at a single mark, but like machine gun fire,
hitting a hundred spots at once. I can only name here the chief
objects for discussion, objects that art, literature, music and the
drama, in common with the speaker, have found to be of prime
value in serving their constituency.

I name sorrow, first. We live in a world hungry for sympathy.
The speaker sometimes wonders why an address, carefully prepared, thoughtful, faultlessly phrased, abounding in interesting
information, and sparkling with wit, meets with so meager a
response. It has been because the hearers have not got what
they needed. They may not have been conscious of their need;
they may not in their thought have asked of the speaker anything but what he offered them. But they were disappointed.
The most efficient salesman is the one that knows what his cus-
tomer needs—even if he has to show him what it is that he
needs—and supplies that. Said Joseph Parker, who filled
London's most prominent pulpit for a generation: "He that
preaches to broken hearts, to tired lives, to disappointed hopes,
preaches to all time." This is as true of any speech as it is of a
sermon. It seems to teach that we like best those that show most
interest in us—but you do, don't you? Perhaps if a speaker says
to others what he most needs to hear himself, he will furnish
them with what they can use. Beecher: "Men who are broken
in heart seek those whose hearts have been broken." Every pain
and disappointment that have broken into your experience
have raised the level of the water of life in your well. The story

is a familiar one of the music teacher who said to a carefree pupil with a fine voice: "If I can bring you some sorrow that will break your heart, I will make you the greatest singer in the world!"

A second element that every formal address should contain is instruction. The fascination of acquiring knowledge is second only to that of imparting it. There is a demand for the teaching function. Every audience is eager to learn. Ignorance is one of the world's prime mischief-makers. Teachers, whether of truth or of folly, readily command a hearing. People turn from those that entertain, even from those that thrill them by their eloquence, to the men that can satisfy their intellectual curiosity about things they have for years been wondering about. But teaching requires tact. New truth is startling, especially to the young. It should be imparted gradually. It is not safe to turn a fire-hose on young plants. New truth provides a hearer with wings, but one should be sure that he knows how to use them. Emancipated slaves may be a source of danger.

The subject of good government needs the defence of the platform. The fact that so much is being said on this subject is one of the reasons why there should be more, of the right sort. The man with an ax to grind, the cynic that harps on the faults of our public officials but does nothing to help them to improve, or to provide more decent successors when their terms expire, the would-be reformer who is for reforming all men but himself, the sincere lover of the public good whose ideals are high but who is unacquainted with the facts, all these roar with thunder that threatens to drown the voice of wisdom. The crooked politician is not dismayed by the sound of his own voice. He loudly demands of the educator and sober advocate of good government that they "let politics alone." Let him first let us alone. There are great questions before us today—inflation, international relationships, racial tensions, church and state, censorship of books, moving pictures and the stage, farm-relief — questions on which, to use the phrase of Carlyle's, "thought once awakened does not again slumber." Everybody is discussing these topics on the streets; let them have clear-eyed, brave discussion by men that have only the public service at heart.

In this heyday of prosperity, men will welcome and follow light on financial questions. Budgets national and domestic, economy in Washington and in the kitchen, local taxation, the tariff, buying on the instalment plan, the stabilization of currency, competition between farmer and middleman, child and female factory labor, are subjects for appraisal in school and congressional debate. The rise of the "university union" is full of promise. The "literary exercises" of the rural school-house, the public forum and small Chautauqua circuit, are national safeguards.

Bring enough individuals together, and you get society. Masses can be made over only by making over the units. Society is not a living organism as Herbert Spencer, in the early days of sociology, seemed to think, but is made up of free and independent men and women. That is the reason why the government depends on the public speech of the voter, farm and factory on the hands, the church and social ethics on the convert. The most important use to which the tongue can be trained is building Christian character. Why in the name of sense, asked Count Tolstoy, are millions spent for the eradication of tuberculosis and yellow fever, and nothing for the cure of *vanity?* The man that talks down the things that are evil, and talks up the things that are good, speaks to lasting purpose. "Let the trumpet," said Calvin, "which sounds for the Lord arrest all who hear by its power and clarity, and let it never give forth an uncertain tone."

3

THE SPEAKER HIMSELF

Because speaking in public is the greatest of the arts, it can be learned. Every one can become an able workman of speech, if he is willing to pay the price. There are no bargains on the counters of life. Sam Jones, the Southern lecturer, said people get what they go after and pay for: "a man goes into a realtor's office, and buys a hundred thousand dollar piece of property; a woman goes into the department store across the street and buys a five cent paper of pins. Both get what they go after." Before any action there must be the will to act; and before the will to act there must be a conviction of the value of the action. That is why the opening chapters of this book have dealt with the importance of public speech. For only to the degree that the student weighs the value of what he is to do will he be driven to proper preparation. If God has called, and the public has seconded the call, God and the public will stand by you.

We often hear the objection: "So many have tried and failed." But if we could read their hearts, we should find that they didn't really care whether they succeeded or not. That is a serious charge to make against them, but everything goes to show that it is justified. The way to succeed is to take the road that leads to success, and keep going till you get there. The reason black Jim failed as a miner was because "he had de gold fever, but he didn't hab de diggin' principle." It is win or die. The ease with which the master works deceives the apprentice. Some thought Demosthenes not a really great orator, because he had to labor so hard. When Pytheas: "All your arguments smell of the lamp," Demosthenes: "Yes, to be sure, but your lamp and mine, my friend, are not witness to the same labors." A successful speech is often called *a gem.* The figure is apt. A speech, like a gem, is given by nature, dug out by man, cleared of clinging mud, cut, polished, set and worn as an extension of personality.

The speaker must prepare every speech thoroughly. Pitfalls abound, at best. Modern audiences are alert and intelligent. When the minister preached at Seamen's Bethel in Boston, and used a ship-illustration, he inquired of one of the old tars afterward: "I hope you liked my sermon?" "Wall, it was all right, except that you fetched your ship into port stern fust." That your word may stand, it is imperative that you be ready in every detail for every occasion. There are no "unimportant" talks.

You must be prepared for your audience's sake. In the study, you are to lay your very soul, in imagination, at the feet of your audience to help and serve them. Wrote the eloquent T. De Witt Talmadge of Brooklyn: "I never preach a sermon without bearing in mind that little word *help.*" The motto of the Boy Scouts is the motto of the creative speaker: "Do something for somebody every day." In 1924, the late Russell H. Conwell announced that his lecture, *Acres of Diamonds,* which was the world's most successful lecture, had been delivered 6,150 times. It brought in twelve million dollars, all of which he gave away, principally to aid in the education of forward-looking young persons. He was eighty-one when he delivered it for the last time. Every word of that lecture had been prepared with the audience in his mind's eye.

The preparation must be thorough, also, for the sake of the subject. It is the speaker's adopted child, and deserves the best nurture and a well-balanced upbringing before being turned out into the world to shift for itself among strangers. To "mean well" is not a substitute for intelligent adaptation to the requirements of the topic in hand. To be sincere does not finish one's responsibility to one's charge.

You must make adequate preparation for your own sake. The advertisement, "Treat yourself to the best," is not altogether selfish. In Herbert Spencer's *Data of Ethics,* the chapter on *Egoism the Truest Altruism* makes it plain that to serve others we must first serve ourselves. You have a standard to maintain. You must be worthy of your self-respect. Perhaps you are by nature a tedious speaker. Thoughts come slowly. Speech halts. Your voice is thin or throaty, your manner timid, your carriage awkward.

Others have faced these obstacles. Dwight L. Moody the great evangelist was advised by the officers of his church, when he began to speak, that since he would never succeed he should not try to talk in public. Many influential leaders in the Senate and at the bar have had to fight a born ineptitude. The very consciousness that nature had done nothing for them in that respect, roused their ambition to do all for themselves. The fact that you know your faults is a point in your favor. Failures seldom do. Because these faults are so impedient and so evident, there is the more reason for effort to vanquish them. "If the iron be blunt, you must put to more strength." If, on the other hand, you are a born speaker, and it is as natural to speak convincingly as it is to breathe, you must beware of neglecting the training which such gifts deserve. Persons possessed with "the fatal gift of eloquence," to use Bismarck's phrase, often play hare to the plodding tortoise. They neglect preparation, trust to their native talent, and fall off the ladder. Valuable jewels are worth polishing.

To prepare speeches, it is essential for the speaker to prepare himself. As an Old Testament writer has put it: "Be thou prepared, yea, prepare thyself." There is a good deal of nonsense talked about "being yourself." Whom else can you be? No masquerade in other men's guise can hide your outline. An audience can see through you as if you were made of plate glass. Ancient Abu Taib was right about it: "No greater disaster can befall a man than to be opened and found to be empty." Every audience has its can-opener, and will soon find out whether there is a worm or a pearl inside. It is a vain hope to try to impart what you don't possess. You are better as you are. If clouds gave sunshine, what should we do for rain? There is endless charm in the varieties of religious experience of Phillips Brooks, Joseph Parker, Rabbi Wise, Fosdick, Bishop Hughes, Robert Speer. An eastern minister so aped the great evangelist that he was called "little Moody." If he had used the implements God gave him, he would not have been called little. There is an evangelist abroad known as Billy Monday: that is going the famous baseball preacher one better!

Cultivate manliness and womanliness: the force of Theodore Roosevelt, or the feminine intuition of Frances Willard. "Manhood is the best sermon." In *manhood,* a somewhat vague term, we understand four qualities: modesty, force, sincerity, courage. People sneer at meekness, as if meekness were weakness. Few have sufficient strength of character or simplicity of nature to be meek. When the young student strode up the center aisle, "carrying his head on his shoulders as if it were the holy sacrament," and after an ignominious failure on the platform slunk with drooping feathers down the side aisle, a discreet old man said to him: "Young feller, if you'd come in the way you went out, you'd a went out the way you come in." True modesty and force are consistent. It is a pitiable sight to see a good man who is in the right give way before a bully who is wrong. To hold convictions without obstinacy, to have force without brutality, to reprove error without cynicism, to be brave without being rash, to triumph without contempt and lose without discouragement, to lead without the love of leadership, to despise crime and love the criminal, to argue a point and stay fair, these are the marks of strength. Platform success is impossible to an insincere man. To mean what you say is to win respect. Sincerity was the crowning trait of Abraham Lincoln, the trait that has made him the model of American life, and given shape to the figure of "Uncle Sam." A young child can tell whether the speaker is telling the truth. The actor's reason for the superior popularity of his profession over that of the unsuccessful minister is as just as it is familiar: "We speak fiction as if it were truth, and you speak truth as if it were fiction." The fourth element of true manliness or womanliness is courage. Beecher said of the minister: "A congregation knows when their minister is afraid of them, just as a horse knows when his driver is afraid of him." The mighty Rowland Hill drew the pregnant distinction between rashness and courage: "Rash preaching disgusts; timid preaching leaves poor souls fast asleep; bold preaching alone is honored of God." Believe in yourself, and in your ability to succeed. Your fit estimate of yourself is to a large degree the standard by which others will measure you.

Let the speaker cultivate the gift of conversation. The ability to talk in private and to talk in public are different gifts. Do not be like the pastor who "was invisible six days, and incomprehensible on the seventh." Ideas become clear when they are transmitted through the medium of conversation. Each will learn to value the other's point of view. It is in conversation that the platform speaker can learn to express himself convincingly. He learns to think in the presence of others. It is in conversation that the speaker can put to the test in the crucible of everyday experience the thoughts on which he meditates for public address. It is in conversation that he finds the pulse of those whose spiritual and mental health he would improve. It is by learning of the needs of those to whom he speaks that the minister and other kinds of public speakers can compound the solaces and cures he has to offer from the platform. The pulpit is kept in vital contact with the only source of its power when the minister spends much time in prayer and meditation; the pulpit is kept in vital touch with those who come before it each Sunday when the minister moves freely about among his people in all hours of the week.

Another paramount factor in self-preparation is select reading. From a score of sources of rain and flood and mountain stream come the waters that fill the reservoir of life-giving irrigation whose ditches and laterals thread the thirsty orchards and gardens of the arid plain. When Dr. Cadman was asked, after one of his lectures at the Pacific School of Religion, how many books he had read in preparation for that course, he replied: "A hundred and fifty." Have more water in your well than you can draw at any one dipping.

The distinction is to be made between general and special reading; the former is capital, the latter is for dividends. Many interesting speakers limit their reading to the subject of the next address. This makes a speech up to date, and bristling with information. But the speaker is little ahead mentally. At the beginning of his career, after every address, he cries to his wife in despair: "I've told all I know: I never can make another speech!" He carries a loaded rifle, but he goes to the front without a cartridge belt. The student that travels afield in several, carefully chosen branches of literature and knowledge becomes more interesting every year. He does not have to "salt" his mine in order to be sure of gold for his coinage. He, more truly than men of any other calling, needs to "know something about everything, as well as everything about something." All is grist that comes to his mill. No matter what he picks up, some day he will have a use for it. The minister, above all, must reserve to himself time for general reading as well as for special study, and let him—and his wife, too—jealously guard those precious periods.

Acquire an appreciation for the beautiful. Cultivate aesthetic taste. Be particular about the pictures you hang on the walls of your home, and about the pictures you hang on the walls of your heart. Each breathes out an atmosphere. Your speeches will take on the spirit of your own refinement. One life breathes emptiness or decay; another, attar of roses. Be high class men and women. Coarseness is not strength. University training in the past has been lamentably weak in the fine arts. Classic music, architecture, painting, statuary, are a sealed book to the average college graduate. The names of Da Vinci, Raphael, Michelangelo, Millet, Sargent, Beethoven, Liszt, Bach, Mozart, Kreisler, Christopher Wren should be at least as familiar to his ears as the names of war heroes and movie stars. The instruments of the orchestra have played as important a part in the development of the race as the instruments of human murder. An Oriental rug costs no more than the much advertised linoleums, and feels more comfortable to the feet and to the eye.

The successful speaker will make himself fit, also, physically. Said Horace Mann: "Not only lying lips, but a dyspeptic stomach is an abomination to the Lord." Build up a robust body. It is the foundation on which both brain and spirit are to stand. When Beecher was asked by a group of Brooklyn ministers what are the qualifications of success in the ministry, he said with a laugh: "Brains, brass, and belly!" Corporeal soundness is certainly not the least material of the speaker's sources of power. Being physically fit is in the long run perhaps worth more than a college education. The idea that to be frail makes one interesting savors of mid-Victorian sentimentality. The reason those who have wrought greatly with frail bodies, like Summerfield, Frances Ridley Havergal, David Brainerd, Robert Louis Stevenson, Chopin, G. D. Boardman, Keats, and others, are so well known to us, is because they are so few. Nearly every great man, and especially a great speaker, has had glorious health—Phillips Brooks, Daniel Webster, D. L. Moody, Lincoln, Spurgeon, Bryan, Sunday, Norwood, Borah, Fosdick—one might almost call the roll of all famous speakers. The uninitiated have no conception of the tremendous drain speaking makes on the physical powers.

I have found a half-hour's address equal to a day's work in the fields. Joseph Parker declared: "Preaching is self-murder; it is shedding of blood." It often takes three days to recover the virtue that goes out of one during an earnest appeal, even when the body is in the pink of condition. A red-blooded Saturday will go far toward saving a blue Monday.

There are five simple rules that are fundamental to the maintenance of good health, and in naming them I hope I shall not seem too paternal in the eyes of those to whom these have long been familiar rules of living. It would have been of value to me and my classmates in Rhetoric if we had had instructions equally explicit. They are:

1. Eight hours' sleep, if possible in the open air; and a fifteen minutes' siesta after luncheon. Where one is to speak twice or oftener the same day, there should be an hour or two of relaxation in sleep between addresses. Henry Ward Beecher used to say that if he did not sleep Saturday night his congregation would on Sunday.

2. A cold plunge or shower on rising, if a good reaction follows.

3. A minimum of six or eight glasses of water daily.

4. Two hours of outdoor exercise each day, except when you have to do an unusual amount of mental work. Lincoln's rail-splitting, Gladstone's ax, Roosevelt's hunting, Taft's golf, "Billy" Sunday's baseball, have built tissue, and set a good example. If such men find time for outdoor exercise, you can. Every professional man should have a wholesome avocation to draw his mind from his regular vocation, and to keep his body fit, a favorite athletic sport or some fixed kind of manual labor. A weazened religionist said reprovingly to a healthy sinner: "Flesh and blood cannot inherit the kingdom of God," to which the other: "Then you're safe, for you have neither."

5. Eat slowly, and not too much. Live moderately, or you will suffer immoderately.

Maintain a fervent inner life, if you would keep within speaking distance of your audience. *Ex nihil, nihil fit.* You cannot impart what you do not possess. What infernal nonsense it is for auditors to say they don't want a speaker to work upon their feelings! It is exactly what we all do want him to do. The emotions are the power plant of the human factory. From them come both our joys and our impulses to action. Human lizards cannot soar. A successful speaker is deeply emotional. Eloquence is born in an atmosphere of feeling. Live in your altitudes, not in your platitudes.

Cultivate your ambition. Who gets what he does not half want? Ambition makes the man. Ambition conquers all things. It stops the mouth of lions, and quenches the violence of the sword. On the tomb of Green, the English historian, are the words: "He died climbing." In the Pacific Electric waiting-room in Los Angeles is a warning sign which has always fascinated me: "This waiting-room is for the traveling public only. Habitual loafing therein is prohibited." What a motto for a college class-room, a store, or a church! This room is for people that are going somewhere! One has said if a piece of iron could speak, it would say: "I am cold, I am black, I am hard." But thrust that iron in the fire, and then what will it say? "My coldness is gone, my hardness is gone, my blackness is gone!" The torch of heaven transforms stagnation into illumination.

4

THE SPEAKER'S RELATION
TO HIS AUDIENCE

The speaker that sincerely serves his audience will make them feel, when he dismisses them, that they owe him a debt of gratitude greater than they can pay. Every such speech is an epoch in a hearer's life. But audiences can be spoiled as easily as children by a weak apologetic air. The "I thank you" of the inexperienced after-dinner speaker, and the "I crave your indulgence for one word more in closing," make the audience feel that they have conferred a favor by coming at all. He was asked:

"Have you ever gone before an audience?"

"I have addressed audiences, but they usually went before I did."

The two prime essentials for any artist are knowledge of his materials and knowing how to use them. No other education, however complete, will atone for ignorance of his audience, on the speaker's part. It is his only cue as to what he is to say, and how he is to say it. The audience is the speaker's lifelong study.

When speech and speaker have been prepared, and the hour of ascending the platform is near, experience will attest the value of the following rules.

1. Between preparation and delivery it is well to rest the mind just before speaking. Some speakers lie down for a nap. An eloquent Southern friend of mine reads a profitable book, on a topic that has no relation to his coming theme. Another listens to phonograph records. Another takes a stroll, or attends an informal religious service. It is dangerous to become over-interested in the coming speech during its preparation. Tolstoy:

33

"It is a well-known fact that no strong emotion can be long sustained." You can't eat your cake and keep it too. The habit of some young speakers of talking their material over with an interested friend, detailing the divisions, etc., is pernicious. Many a good speech has been talked to death before it was spoken. The mind is like an elastic: the farther away you pull it, the bigger the snap when it comes back. At the same time, one must beware of exciting diversions during the opening exercises, to pull the mind away. Center your attention on the approaching speech.

2. After rising to speak, when you walk to the front of the platform, wait a moment till the audience gets through coughing and moving about. This will give you time to compose yourself, as you look over the assembly. It will draw their attention to the opening sentences, which are often, and always should be, of special importance. To feel a dread before speaking, when "within scorching distance of the fire of criticism," is not a hindrance to success; on the contrary, it is a valuable asset. Sheppard: "The apprehensive temperament is like nervousness, bad for one's happiness, but good for one's speaking." Shakespeare: "Security is mortals' chiefest enemy." Mental security makes the "fatal seventh" in baseball. The secret of the second speech of the day, which has proved such a mystery to many, rests on good psychology. To win a triumph in the morning is to court failure at night, through over-confidence. Your mind is not on the evening appointment: it is on the morning victory. Whereas, if you fail on the first occasion, you are more than likely to be rewarded by making a clean sweep at night. Before honor goeth humility. The world's best speakers usually have a sinking feeling before speaking. "Demosthenes, Cicero, Curran, Chalmers, Erskine, Pitt, Gladstone, Disraeli, Mirabeau, Patrick Henry, Clay, Gough, Beecher, Salvini, Henry Irving, Richard Mansfield, and many others, were subject to stage fright."

3. Have the opening sentences and the introductory thoughts at your tongue's end, whether what you are to utter is a speech, a rally cheer, an announcement, or a court sentence. Hesitation at the beginning destroys the hearers' confidence. They expect you to know what you are about. Walk slowly when you rise and step forward to your speaking place. Be master of yourself,

your subject, your audience. Fasten your mind on their needs, not on yours.

4. Form the habit of regarding your audience in the light of agreeable companions, whom you are eager to know. Don't be afraid of them. Both for their sakes, and also for yours, they would rather have you succeed in your speech than not. They are not critical, but genuinely friendly, in their attitude. They are far more likely to be critical of a veteran speaker than of a beginner in the art. Enjoy them, and they will enjoy you. They have come with that purpose. A slip of the tongue, or other gaucherie, is often a point of connection. Such things are actually assumed, at times, by old speakers, for the sake of their favorable impression, and to emphasize the thing that is to follow. Respect your audience. Don't "talk down" to them, particularly if you are addressing an ignorant group, or crowd of newsboys. It is a compliment to an audience to treat them with respect, and tends to make them worthy of it. If you use slang anywhere, let it be before professors, judges, or ministers. A young Harvard graduate whom I knew, beginning his ministry in a Colorado saloon town, used in his sermons the language of his hearers, and they ran him out of town. Take your audience into your confidence. One remembers the three speakers, one of whom talked at his hearers, one to them, and the third for them. Hold converse with them. Treat them like a family, without familiarity. Illustrations from personal experience help in this, but they must be given without self-consciousness. An audience does not generally like a speaker to talk about himself. Montaigne was half right: "A man never speaks of himself without loss." He is supposed to be more interested in something else. One of the most profitable concepts that you can form, and one that you should always bear in mind, is that public speaking is conversation, and subject to the same laws; except that it is in a larger room, the speaker is standing up, speaking in a louder voice, to more persons, in a more dignified manner, and does all the talking himself. This thought will relieve you of embarrassment, make you more natural in both voice and bearing, and put your audience at ease. Professionalism, except in a hopeless snob, is impossible in private conversation. Strangers have become neighbors to you. Study

Beecher's famous address at Liverpool on the attitude of England toward our Civil War. It changed him from a target into a comrade. Old-fashioned "oratory" has given way, like so much similar artificial splendor of two generations back, to the plain speaking of public conversation.

5. Look your audience in the eye. "Negativism" is a well-known psychological defect arising from weakness of character. The eye holds an audience, and each individual in it, like a lariat. Similar to the directing thrust of the orchestra leader's baton to groups all around him, it seems to say: "Now, *you* get in!" Bashfulness has lost its worth in our frank day; it is rated as cowardice. While M. Bautain, France's famous preacher, said he kept his gaze just above the heads of his hearers, lest their faces should make him forget what he was thinking about, it is only the exceptional speaker who can so ignore direct eye-contact with his audience and still succeed. I have seen timid speakers fasten their eyes on a distant spot in the upper corner of the auditorium, and keep it nailed there from beginning to end. While this is fatal to an effective hold upon an audience, it is only slightly less foolhardy to fix one's glittering eye, like that of the Ancient Mariner, on a few individuals, to the neglect of the rest. Suppose one of them should yawn, or whisper? Some hearers try to make the speaker look at them, to show their power over him. Your eye is your own private property.

Don't think you have failed if somebody falls asleep. A student of audiences knows that "sitting down, itself, is a partial relaxation," especially after an active day spent in the fresh air. Sleep is most liable to be induced by excitement, or unusual interest. It may be a compliment! A San Francisco lawyer, according to a press report, was thus afflicted, and once, when held up by a gunman, instantly fell asleep. The bandit, with profound admiration: "A man that's got a nerve like that, don't owe me anything!" A Western ministerial friend of mine complained to one of his church trustees that he would warrant that the latter had not fallen asleep on the front bench at the minstrels, Saturday night! (He did not suspect that he had actually been there.) The trustee retaliated: "No, pastor, I didn't; and if you'll make your sermons as interesting as those minstrels were, I'll keep awake in church." It is not necessary, however, always to follow in the footsteps of Al Jolson. Let the speaker derive comfort from the fact that the prophet Daniel fell asleep while the angel Gabriel was preaching. The Reverend Jonathan Swift expressed regret that the example of the youth Eutychus, who fell out of the window and broke his neck while asleep, during a sermon of the apostle Paul, had not seemed to serve as a warning to his successors.

6. The speaker must take a lively personal interest in his introduction. There is only one way to do this, and that is to make the introduction interesting enough to deserve it. A speech, like an automobile, must be started right. Listlessness is contagious. The thing must start in an alert manner, the speaker standing on both feet in strong and easy attitude. The introduction sets the pace. Announcement of subject—or text, if a sermon—should be varied. It rests a congregation to have a preacher break the old conventional form, and begin with the words: "Ladies and gentlemen," "The motto for our thinking," or some other dignified, and yet fresh and natural approach to his theme. Life is as dignified as death. Don't begin with an apology, unless something extraordinary has happened. Kleiser: "An apology is weakness on parade." A disappointed auditor complained that a speaker "spent half his time in saying he was not prepared and the other half in proving it." Mr. Beecher said he never spoke disparagingly of his own sermons: there were plenty of others to do that. The audience looks up to the speaker with respect. Maintain a certain superiority to your audience. For the time being, and in what you have to say, you are the master, and they are the followers. Remember throughout, of course, that the Master of us all stooped to wash His disciples' feet.

7. If you find yourself stuck in the middle of a sentence, or have stage fright, or forget what is coming next, go right on talking. Remember that pioneer preacher, entangled in a forest of words, thicker than the woods in which he was preaching, who suddenly paused: "Brethren, I've forgot the subject of this sentence, and lost the predicate, but—I'm bound for the kingdom of heaven!" God directed Saint Peter: "Be not afraid, but speak." Fortunately, the mind is naturally logical, even to the degree that it sometimes makes the speaker forget ("on purpose," as the

Freudians would say) a paragraph because it is in the wrong place; and later recalls it in toto when the argument is ready for it. Every speaker has had this happen to him. Memory is a faithful servant, and she responds loyally to the trust that is placed in her. Frequently the mind, in the warmth of action, kindles brand new thought that is far better than what has been forgotten. That is the reason that lectures improve with the telling. Irrelevant matter is seen to be what it is; and each sudden inspiration is preserved and set in its lustrous place. Whitefield, the most impassioned evangelist in the history of the church, said that he could not do justice to a sermon until he had preached it fifty times.

8. Go after your audience and get them. Emerson defined eloquence as "a taking sovereign possession of the audience." When a man talks to hear himself talk, he talks in such a way that nobody else wants to hear him talk. The old whaler, listening to a sentimental discourse, complained that the indecisive speaker "had no harpoon." The very word *delivery* implies that some one gets what you say. A strong speech is one that makes its hearers strong. A speaker may be surrounded by people, and yet not find one of them. How can he find what he is not really looking for?

Have the will to win. Men will brush you aside and pass you on the road, who are your inferiors in every respect but this one. We hear persons say: "So-and-So has no talent, but he has force." What is force but one of the first of talents? It deserves its high reward. The man that does not will to win might as well have willed to fail. For failure waits for him. To strive for success, is success. Fame, wealth, friends, may be wanting; but the man himself will not be found wanting who, when the curtain falls, shall be able to say: "I have striven with all my heart to bring cheer and strength to my fellows." Ella Wheeler Wilcox wrote:

> "There is no chance, no destiny, no fate,
> Can circumvent, or hinder, or control
> The firm resolve of a determined soul."

5

THE MATERIAL SETTING

Two sayings of great military leaders, which I read as a boy in French authors, have often proved helpful to me: "We must fear the enemy afar off, in order no longer to fear him when near at hand"; and, similarly, "A general may indeed be conquered, but he must never suffer himself to be surprised." There is many a factor of a successful speech that is not included in the speech, and that may become a source of disaster if it is not given attention beforehand, that

> "little rift within the lute
> That bye-and bye will make the music mute,
> And ever widening, slowly silence all."

What a difference the right frame makes for a picture! Not only do different pictures require different frames, suitable to them, but styles of framing differ from one period of time to another. Since the mind craves variety, but has not the talent to provide it beyond a limited range, styles of a hundred years ago return and go out again, from century to century. The young married couple with good taste will consult the best art store in town for appropriate framing for their pictures, though they can have them framed elsewhere. This well-known principle is applicable to the material setting for a speech, or for a long succession of speeches. Like a gem, its brilliance and attractiveness will hang somewhat on the setting by which it is enclosed. The Japanese, the most aesthetic civilized nation in the world, study with care the standpoint from which a landscape is to be photographed, sometimes so arranging the landscape that only the most favorable spot is available for the tourist to see it from. They trim a tree to please the eye of the observer from underneath. The ancient Greek added an entasis to his columns, and a bulge to his temple steps; and placed the ornamentation within easy range of the eye, and not out of sight at the top, as American architects do.

A few rules will suffice for most occasions and situations in which speech is to be made. If it is outdoors, as in the case of a funeral service, a Fourth of July address, etc., select carefully your place to stand, with relation to where the audience is to be. How carefully Jesus arranged the sitting of the five thousand before ministering to their physical needs! To adapt one's self to a situation prepared for a quite different purpose is a severe strain on both orator and auditors. I heard "Billy" Sunday in a prizefight ring in Los Angeles, whose large square platform was surrounded on all sides by the great crowd, requiring him to walk round and round continually, in order to face each section in turn. Presently, he exclaimed: "Seventh round! Wow! I'm tired!" He left the ring exhausted, after muscular exercise that would have retained for Jack Dempsey the championship. Wherever your speech is to be, go in beforehand, when possible and look the situation over.

If indoors, make sure, before the audience come in, of good circulation of air. Our fathers of the last generation, believing that fresh air was perilous to health, slept will all windows down and heavy curtains to their beds. The average sexton appears to share their dread. The dullness of a lecture or other speech has been laid to the speaker, when only the janitor was to blame. Candidates for a political office or a church pastorate have undoubtedly sometimes been rejected on account of poor ventilation. It was not their remarks that were stale and unoriginal, but the air. A farmer, or any one else who is accustomed to living in the open, cannot keep awake in moribund air. The effect of ventilation is as vital on the speaker as it is on his hearers. Lack of fresh air is one of the chief causes of the deadly anti-climax. When Spurgeon transferred his congregation temporarily into a huge public structure in London, he asked his trustees to improve the pent-up ventilation. As they were slow about it, he went in on a week-day, and poked out a row of windows with his cane. If draughts prevail in the auditorium, let the usher ask the sensitive person to move his seat, rather than to kill the enjoyment of all the rest. Modern buildings are provided with elaborate systems of ventilation by scientific circulation of fresh outside air. Where such expensive system is not available, some plan may be adopted which shall take account of nature's law that warm air rises and cool air descends. An opening at the apex of the ceiling, boards in front of the bottom of the windows, vents around the base of the platform, are often effective.

Lighting of public meeting-places has received a vast amount of intelligent study. The old-time central chandelier with its cascade of local illumination has given way to indirect or distributed lights. A brilliant room affords a sense of cheer, and satisfies the near-sighted. Adequate lighting is worth all it costs. "Dim religious light" tends to make one irreligious, though it may further secret courting. St. Paul was converted by a "light above the brightness of the sun." There should never be a light behind the speaker. It has an hypnotic effect upon those that have to face it; in fact, to fix the eyes upon a light, even dim, is one of the devices used by hypnotists to beget eye-strain with a view to inducing hypnosis. By neuropathic physicians it is prescribed for insomnia during the night. If there is a window back of the speaker, or white wall, it can be covered. The platform may be satisfactorily lighted by foot-lights, by ceiling lighting, or by a screened desk-lamp.

In determining the seating of a building, it is important that the auditorium should not be too large for the size of the probable congregation, unless there are sliding partitions that will provide for special crowds, or the reverse. Adapt the number of permanent seats to actual needs. Their construction must be studied with a view to comfort. It may be the only comfort that some hearers will get. Besides having greater dignity, pews are more practical in a church than opera chairs, as they hold more, and are easier to sit on. A church should be furnished with churchly furniture. Avoid a center aisle, at least for more than half way up the room. Its only advantage is for weddings, which are infrequent. Funerals are more satisfactorily conducted without the center aisle, enabling the procession to pass up one side aisle, and down the other. The center aisle makes a chasm in the audience directly in front of the speaker, forcing him to talk down a lane.

The speaker will learn, sometimes by bitter experience, to meet unexpected distractions. A thoughtless sexton is a constant menace to the spirit of worship. The phrase, "a well-meaning man," designates a man that is always doing what he doesn't mean to do. The opening sentences of an address are his favorite moment for prowling about in full view of the audience. He imagines that, by holding his head down, he makes himself invisible. It really serves only to make him run into things. The inexperienced young speaker is his meat. He hopes that what is really a determination on his part to attract attention away from the speaker to himself will be regarded as a burning desire to be useful. The late Dr. J. Q. A. Henry, preaching in the First Baptist Church in Denver, spoke poetically of "angel footsteps on the stairs," and by way of accompaniment, apparently, the janitor, who I should judge wore thirteens, descended the stairs beside the pulpit with steps that echoed throughout the large church. It is wise for clergymen to take a thorough course of training for their profession, but the sexton needs it more. His friendly services, wisely directed, are an invaluable aid to good order. Let the minister train his sexton, but not during the hour of service, nor in front of a waiting audience.

Then there are the animals. Any public speaker of two or three years' experience could write a book on the distractions caused to the student in college or to the devout in church by the ingenious activities of tame beasts. Why do scientific investigators spend their money in the jungles of Africa studying the psychology of lower forms of zoological life, when the house of God is available? In the case of insects, it is not their ceaseless activity that causes disturbance; it is the intermitting movements. Instructions to ushers should include earnest directions to keep an eye open for all forms of animal and insectivorous life.

What shall be the speaker's attitude toward babies? An irritable man may do irreparable hurt to the feelings of loyal parents by publicly ordering them, as some do, to take that baby out. It isn't the crying or laughing of infants that disturbs a public gathering, but it is their bewitching cunningness. Over a half dozen rows of seats in all directions, words of wisdom from the platform get no heed. Modern churches are provided with a nursery, where babies receive care from competent nurses during the service. When this is not provided, the mother may choose a seat near the door, and walk out for a few moments with her child. Many a mother has missed all public gatherings for a good part of her married life on account of her dread of disturbing others.

A less necessary disturbance to the speaker, but one that demands tactful handling, is misbehavior, laughing and whispering, on the part of callow persons that have come, not to hear, but to enjoy each other's society. It will not do to ignore such rudeness, lest it become habitual, and contagious. It may be effectually and permanently checked, without offence, by a wise usher. As has been pointed out, the speaker must be master of the situation, always, or retire in defeat. Never lose your temper, or get petty or nervous. The very fact that you have the advantage will militate against you. Sickness or other causes may make it necessary for persons to withdraw, even at the most critical moment. Better too much patience, than too little.

Strange to say, distractions are sometimes an asset. They may be seized upon and turned to advantage. They afford just that human touch that creates a sympathetic interest between the speaker and his audience; and if he is alive to his opportunity, he will make the most of them. When the witty Poindexter S. Henson was lecturing in a large hall, a window-blind somewhere in the spaces above him gave way and fell with a loud crash, just as he was introducing his lecture. He said: "I've begun to bring down the house already." The audience was his, from that moment. Lloyd George is renowned for his ability at repartee, a weapon that English audiences delight to call forth, and sometimes wish they hadn't. When he began an address with the words, "I am here—," a voice from the gallery called out, "So am I!" to which, when the laughter subsided a bit, he rejoined: "Yes, but you're not all there!" When, however, through one's own mistakes, such as a slip of the tongue, the serious thought of the congregation is diverted hopelessly into a burst of merriment, there is no resource for the speaker but to pause, with an understanding smile, till the waves subside. Even then, the effect of the address may be deepened by thus incidentally establishing a fresh point of contact.

It is evident, from what has been said in this chapter, that ushers are vitally correlated to the material setting. Their cooperation and their individual initiative have been too often left to chance, by fallacious neglect on the part of those in charge. Like all healthy men, they are looking for a chance to be useful. It is a prevalent but false idea that all mankind are like the lowest, in seeking to do as little for the general welfare as possible. The contrary is the fact, in the case of most persons. It is inactivity that makes men unhappy and restless, as well as being a source of annoyance. Give the usher all he can do, and he will shine at his work. In every organization where public gatherings feature, there should be regular meetings of the ushers for discussion of their important task, in all its bearings.

It makes for reverence, and for the dignity of their office, to see that the ushers are dressed suitably in cutaway coats with a flower in the lapel; and that they display a courtesy that studies the comfort of every attendant. They are a shield to the conductor of the service. They are taught to feel their responsibility. There should be a signal beside the speaker's chair, by which he can summon the chairman of the ushers' board. Why should late comers have obtrusive privileges in disturbing those that wish to hear what is going on? In a church service there should be a fixed understanding that no one is to be admitted during prayer, reading of the Scriptures, and solo. The pastor will have it understood that he is to allow a few moments before each of these exercises for late comers to be seated.

The material setting involves a suitable structure in which to meet. Remarkable improvement in the architecture of such buildings has signalized the opening of the present century. Especially has this been true of church architecture. Glorious cathedrals are rising in great centers, like St. John's in New York City, and the cathedral of Saints Peter and Paul in our national capital, that are in every way equal to the matchless piles of medieval England. All over the country, as if by some preconcerted agreement, Colonial church buildings, as perfect as the best of our proud New England types, are being reared. Here and there for the smaller congregation one finds satisfying replicas of the cruciform English country church, in permanent ivied stone. The mosque-like little square churches, many of them after the model of a crematory, are, fortunately for public taste, gradually giving way to these nobler forms. Nobler, because they appeal to the innate sense of the beautiful, and because they inspire the spirit of worship. Gothic and colonial forms may be adapted fully to modern demands by harmonious cloisters and wings, without neutralizing the churchly feeling. Glorious stained glass windows breathe a glow in keeping with the mystical spirit, and at the same time contribute to the sense of the beautiful in worship. Every city should have in at least one steeple or campanile a melodious chime of bells. Private means will take pride in providing such windows and chimes as family memorials.

A nation has to reach mature age, and attain a sufficient degree of financial prosperity before it can take time to be interested in art centers or objects of beauty per se. That age and degree of prosperity have now been attained in America. "In the coming years Washington should be not only the art center of our own country, but the art center of the world." We are beginning to see noble public galleries of painting and sculpture, like that bequeathed by the late Henry E. Huntington, and imposing monuments and types of architecture, taking their place beside our great public libraries ministering to the elevation of public taste. Aesthetic culture, as has been evidenced in many a European capital, is not a substitute for moral training, but may be its handmaid.

The problem of acoustics—like that of a practical chimney-flue —has received much professional study. There are certain well-known principles now familiar to the best architects that will serve the voice of the speaker in public, instead of fighting it as has so often been the case in the history of buildings for general assembly. Building committees have been so frequently discouraged by wretched acoustics, that they have sometimes suspected a sort of magic about the whole thing. I have heard it solemnly declared that two buildings may be built, exactly alike in every respect, in one of which you can hear, and in the other you cannot. Innumerable are the dour effects produced. In one of the finest Presbyterian churches in the West, a huge flag has been suspended above the middle of the room, to break the ebb and flow of the sound waves. The sounding-board, the magna-vox, the pew telephone, are familiar devices.

It is strange that a building devised for ancient Roman courts should have served during all the Christian centuries as the church model, both in shape and in its hideous plainness. While it was a dictum of Ruskin's that artistic decoration and beauty of line are out of place in such a structure as a railroad station, where travelers are always in a hurry with their minds on other matters, the opposite should be true of a building dedicated to public speaking. Here the eye travels about the structure before the address (and frequently while it is in progress), and a chill bare barn of an audience room deadens sensibly the spirits and adds a burden to the speaker's and hearer's shoulders which they should not have to bear. Inside and out, everything should appeal to the eye by its neatness and charm of color and form. Even a humble country church may have its "clean-up day." A week is set apart every year at the time of the celebration of the fall of the Bastille, in Tahiti, when everybody paints, rakes, clips and burns, mends and plants, till the little town of Papeete shines like some Venus coming out of the sea. It is an ambition devoutly to be wished for that a building committee emulate the beauty-loving South Sea islanders in this respect. The interior color scheme may be submitted to a professional decorator, whom the large furnishing stores are glad to send out for this purpose. In general it may be said that the shading, whatever tints are chosen, should grow from dark to light as it ascends from the floor upward—as nature does. The State Churches of Europe set a laudable example to us on this side of the water by their mosaic pictures, and also in the paintings of Scriptural scenes with which they embellish the walls. I wonder whether the great Teacher, if He entered some of our houses of worship, would not exclaim in wrath, as He looked upon their tawdry and cheap untidiness, "Take these things hence!" A certain visiting minister, of whom my mother told me, seemed to have caught that spirit. He had been warned by the timid pastor for whom he was to speak, not to notice that a window beside the pulpit recess was broken, and that the pulpit Bible was in tatters. He did not commit himself; but, just before speaking, he pulled a rag out from a shelf in the pulpit and elaborately stuffed it into the broken window; and, as he announced his text, brought his fist down on the Bible in a way to scatter its pages broadcast over the platform.

His text might well have been, "The Word of God is not bound." The pastor felt pleased with the practical repairs that met his eye on his return.

We echo the Psalmist's prayer, "that I may dwell in the house of Jehovah, to behold the beauty of Jehovah." And as we study the material surroundings of the preacher, the old familiar hymn lines are wafted into memory:

> "I love Thy church, O God!
> Her walls before Thee stand
> Dear as the apple of Thine eye,
> And graven on Thine hand."

6

AUDIENCES AND THEIR WAYS

An audience is to a speaker what the bank is to business: it is the medium by which ideas are kept in circulation. The audience is the speaker's first consideration. His success or failure depends upon his knowledge of it and his adaptation to it. Every speech is a medium of exchange, where the speaker invests his mental capital in escrow, and the audience return to him their dividends of appreciation and support. Each thus contributes to the other. The audience is his farm land, to be cultivated so as to produce a valuable harvest. It is his raw material, out of which he is to construct a finished product for the service of mankind. It is his tool, to wield for the building of public institutions, or for surgery on the body politic. It is his battle ax and weapons of war, without which the enemies of the public weal cannot be driven off. An audience is like a foreign land: he that expects to visit it with pleasure or profit must study its features before he arrives, until he is familiar with its arts and sciences, its history, its possible future, its glories and its Hall of Shame. So must he have the audience in vision, before he has it in sight. The speaker's most insidious temptations have to do with the audience. It is evident that he must have one, and therefore that he must take pains to get it. The larger the better; therefore he must take pains to increase it. Yet it is destructive to his success to seek a large audience primarily for its numbers.

The audience is essential to him. Without an audience, training in public speaking, or an ambition to succeed, would be nugatory. As illustration of this in life's supreme calling, note that all of the titles given to the minister of religion are based upon his relation to his auditors: shepherd, minister, orator, elder, bishop (meaning from its Greek derivation *overseer*), pastor, prophet, teacher—they are all social titles. It is not enough for a speaker to know men as individuals, he must know them in the mass, he must have knowledge of crowds as such, their reactions to social relations, the mob-spirit. Group psychology has not hitherto received the attention it demands. There are reactions, moods, impulses, that characterize a group, that are distinct from those that characterize an individual. Group-psychology is the speaker's study. People behave differently with others from the way they behave when alone.

Further than that, audiences differ radically from one another. Why do audiences show certain characteristic traits, shifting moods, like individuals? The same audience behaves differently at one time from the way it behaves at another time.

An audience has its moods. You can feel them "in the air." They may be alert, dull, intelligent, apathetic, pleasure-seeking, earnest, inquiring, satiated, and—but rarely—critical. The following characterization, by the Rev. J. A. Rondthaler, of various kinds of churches is so descriptively accurate that I include it for my readers' enjoyment:

> "Churches have not only a denominational flavor, but an individuality of atmosphere also. There are noisy, boisterous churches, and sedate and sleepy churches. There are churches which, like sand heaps or jack-straws, fall apart when the benediction is pronounced, and there are churches like mountains that are knit together into a solid fellowship. There are churches that make you involuntarily turn up your collar in midsummer and churches that warm you like a genial hearth-fire in midwinter. I have known churches that have thawed out an icicle in the pulpit and churches that have frozen out a whole procession of ministers. You go into some churches and you wonder whether your clothes fit; and you go into other churches and you wonder whether your heart is right. Some jolt you on the heavenward road as over a badly ballasted railway, and some carry you happily and smoothly as in a palace car. There are churches that make you look around, and there are churches that make you look up. There are some that feed your vanity, and some that make you hunger and thirst after righteousness. Out of some you go without a single inspiration, and out of others you come with the ardent wish for a thousand tongues to tell the old, old story, and for a thousand hands to help the weary and heavy-laden."

The material surroundings are sometimes responsible for these differences. A cold building chills the body, and a cold body chills the mind. The speaker's attitude, specially during his introduction, often creates or changes the atmosphere of an assembly, as a smile or a frown will change the feelings of a family at the breakfast table. The audience is a sort of mirror, in which the speaker sees himself. He shapes them somewhat as a potter shapes his clay, making due allowances always for the nature and state of the clay. Sometimes a speaker and his audience take turns in ruling and following each other. One or the other has the ascendency.

The hour at which a meeting is assembled also makes a marked difference in the feelings of an audience. Every one has felt the difference between a morning and an evening appointment. The old-fashioned New England afternoon church service, held often after a big country dinner, attracted an exceedingly insensible group to stir. If a speaker may be "too full for utterance," a congregation may be too full for audience. A speaker on a program has also to live down or live up to the preceding speaker. The audience has been led somewhere, and he has either to keep them there, to bring them back, or to lead them farther. It makes for his success if he differs strongly in temperament and treatment from his predecessor, providing he maintain the general unity of the program. His exordium, or introduction, is often suggested in such cases by what the last speaker has said. It is like the railroad coupler, which holds two cars together, though they may be as diverse as a passenger coach and a baggage car. If he be too flattering to the preceding speaker, or be suspected to be jealous of his success, he loses his case at the beginning. An audience's judgment is astute in such matters.

It is an interesting fact in the study of social assemblies that there are often emotional centers in a congregation, and these may aid or hinder the speaker's success. He is fortunate that can start such whirlpools of sympathetic feeling as shall spread waves of emotional power to large areas of the house. Sometimes, however, these centers are like sun-spots that appear to affect the weather unfavorably. A new hat, a rich visitor, or an opinionated baby may take charge, to the delight of everyone but the one on the platform. On the other hand, an enthusiast may be of more service to the occasion than the speaker himself. Strong feeling is eminently contagious. B. Fay Mills narrates in *God's*

World a remarkable instance of such influence on the part of a group of saintly officials who suddenly entered the room in a series of meetings that had been all the week up to that night without power to move the attendants. As these men, well known in the city, who had been "on their faces" in prayer came in, Mr. Mills tells us that "a wave of power" swept over the audience, which was distinctly felt throughout the house, and which produced extraordinary effects upon many lives, by their own subsequent testimony. There are *key men* in many an assembly that have an influence that weighs more than a half-dozen rows of seats of the rank and file. Coal gives out more heat when afire than stubble. These regnant individuals often terrify a beginner. A row of ministers may give stage fright to a young preacher. One of the first things to be learned in this art is to be indifferent to the personnel of one's audience, as far as having respect of persons is concerned. They may need help more than their less prominent neighbors; and the fact that he is there to serve the needs of his hearers will make him superior to any terror their presence may inspire. If the White House caught fire, the firemen would not hesitate to play the hose on the blaze because the President of the United States was present. There is one case, however, in which the fear of the judgment of learned or famous hearers is fully warranted, and that is when the speaker has "trusted to luck" as a substitute for preparation. Such indolence will meet its reward.

Not only is there a variety in audiences, but there is a variety in each audience. The Creator never made two things alike. No two blades of grass, no two leaves, no two persons have been replicas. Star differeth from star in glory. Some hearers disappoint, some surprise, some uplift the speaker. The value of a congregation rests, as in a cornfield, on the ears. How these differ! Some are large and full; some blasted with the East wind; some are seed-corn; some, nubbins. The Bible finds ears that are "punctured" (Exod. 21.6); blood-tipped (Exod. 29.20) as if to suggest the spirit of sacrifice; anointed (Lev. 14.28) as if to make regal choice of what shall be admitted to their court; stopped (Prov. 21.13). In Bunyan's *Holy War*, the town of Mansoul is stormed at Ear Gate. So is every man-soul. The audience is human, painfully, delightfully human. We find support in

the sympathetic hearer, who limits his criticism to his own defects. There is a distinction between sympathy and pity, that
is often lost sight of in literature. The sympathetic hearer makes
a good speaker better; the pitying hearer makes a poor one worse.
In pity, the world over, there is an ingredient of contempt. It
would be well for chronic complainers to remember this. There
is a savage instinct in humanity that drives us to pursue the
coward. A sympathetic speaker makes a sympathetic audience.
There is, perhaps in the next seat, the opposing hearer, who
saith in his heart: "Whatever this man has to propose, I'm agin
it!" When a young preacher asked Mr. Spurgeon what he ought
to do about the man in his congregation that kept his fingers in
his ears while he was preaching, the President of the Preachers'
College suggested: "I should pray the Lord to make a fly light on
the end of the man's nose." Next, sits the hungry hearer that
has come from home to get something valuable that he can carry
back with him. He deserves his mileage. Lecturers have an advantage over other speakers in this respect, that persons who
have paid to get in make better listeners. But every speaker is
like the farmer's wife: he likes to "see people take hold." They
are a compliment to his provisions. He soon comes to have the
intelligence of the mother bird which, among a nestful of open
mouths, knows which really is hungry. Such auditors are his
delight. "The full soul loatheth the honeycomb; but to the
hungry soul every bitter thing is sweet."

No part of the address should bear the label of the Dead
Letter Office: "Not called for." Every sentence should fit in
somewhere. There are now on the market patent fertilizers to
stimulate every part of the orange tree; one for making wood,
one for fruit, etc., etc. So every section of the speech is adapted
to somebody's eclectic requirements. It does most, however, for
the cooperative hearer. Books on Public Speaking have paid
too little attention to the hearers. They have emphasized the
man behind the desk, and forgotten the man in front of it, who
often needs the more sympathy. It takes two to make a speech,
the man that speaks and the man that listens. The cooperative
hearer is a propagandist. He is a witness, not only with his eyes,
but with his lips. He is the speaker's Commercial Traveler, his
Extension Course. He bears on tireless wing the pollen from

flower to flower. Ten times one is ten. The speaker adds thought to thought; this hearer multiplies them. To stir the heart of this winged-footed Mercury is therefore the speaker's primary aim.

An address must be framed to reach all of these classes, as the skilled organist uses all the stops. Many roles must be performed by a single speech. It must find a man where he is, and lead him somewhere else. It must adjust itself to the physically deaf in the front and to the mentally deaf in the rear. Men are what you find them; they become what you make them. They catch the speaker's spirit. The change that is wrought in character or point of view is often affected more by what the speaker feels than by what he says. It is a truth of the profoundest significance that

THE AUDIENCE IS THE ECHO OF THE SPEAKER.

There is a world of psychology in the old fable of the boy on the farm that came back from the hills to his mother in tears of rage: "I whistled and a boy that was hiding whistled too." We shouted:

> " 'Who are you?'
> 'Who are you?'
> 'You are mean!'
> 'You are mean!'
> 'I hate you!'
> 'I hate you!' "

His mother explained that it was an echo, and said: "Now, if you'll go back and tell that boy that he is a fine chap and that you love him, you will be surprised at what he will tell you." That tale illustrates better than anything else what I am saying. The audience is your echo. If you are stiff and formal, so they will be. If you take no interest in them, they will have none for you. If your purpose is to help them, if you feel a genuine affection and lively interest in them, they will be all you crave. The audience is the speaker's echo!

7

THE VOICE

Part 1

Three things are said to indicate the superiority of man to the lower animals. These are reason, the making and using of tools, and the gift of language. In sight and hearing in physical strength and agility, they are our superiors. And they possess a voice of both sweetness and volume, without which language would be impossible. But nature has given to man a range and variety of tone vastly beyond the best voices of animals. The human voice has become a matchless instrument, not only in song on the operatic stage, but to a yet greater degree in public speech. There are finer modulations of tone, and more melodious to the ear, on the rostrum than in the concert hall.

A good voice, under the full control of its user, is a necessity to almost all branches of modern life, to the lawyer, promoter, preacher, politician, professor, lecturer, auctioneer, excursion conductor, traffic officer, broadcaster, actor, singer, nurse, labor leader, athletic coach. The voice is receiving special attention from science. It has been restored to many unfortunates that had lost it. Five hundred at least in the United States are now talking through artificial larynxes. Dr. Harvey A. Fletcher, of the Bell Telephone laboratories of New York, its inventor, has restored through this instrument, like a pipe, the power of speech to pathologic sufferers. It is a sort of vocal syphon conveying, from one end inserted through a hole into the chest, to the other end held in the mouth, the air from the lungs. In comparison with this, how small is the effort required by the student of vocal culture! One has only to witness the struggles of his friends who are afflicted with loss of the voice, to realize the value of what we take for granted.

Voice has a magic effect. It wields a strong physical influence, in itself, apart from the significance of the words spoken. The comparison to music is a familiar one, some asserting that the influence of music is intellectual, like mathematics; others, that it is spiritual, or emotional; but the thrill that one feels at the concourse of musical notes is unquestionably physical in part, setting up a vibration of the nerves. That the singer himself depends almost entirely upon the sound is evident from the fact that he appears to be indifferent whether the audience understands the words or not. Certain voices are soothing, others inspiring. It is well-known that persons too deaf to comprehend a word like to hear great orators for the mere sound of their voices. Beecher's voice was not strong; but "there was in it the oratorical timbre which stirs an audience to its depths." It is an encouragement to those with naturally poor voices to remember that Beecher when he was young was worried by a vocal defect that he was afraid would make speaking in public impossible; but when he reached college a teacher of elocution helped him overcome his weakness. From Demosthenes to Roosevelt, men born with weak voices have by diligent effort not only overcome their handicap but have become powerful orators. Beecher himself worked with resolute zeal to perfect his voice, practicing daily the sounds of the vowels, until it grew to be the marvelous instrument that thrilled the world. It is said that the great Whitefield could pronounce the word *Mesopotamia* in such a way as to melt an audience to weeping.

Some persons have been richly gifted by nature with superlative voices. It is probable that many glorious voices have been lost to the world for want of the opportunity to cultivate or to use them. The low register has the best carrying power. A deep-sea bass, low baritone or contralto, can be heard without effort in a conversational tone throughout a great auditorium. Such voices are the delight of the deaf. But it is to be remembered that intensity of conviction and earnestness of purpose, plus having something significant to say, will make of anyone's voice an instrument of communication to which men and women will attend. A distinguished professor of economics at a mid-

Western university is invited to lecture on three continents, but stutters in almost every sentence he utters. Let the speaker work hard to develop the equipment he has, but let nothing which he lacks in vocal quality deter him from bringing to others the truth that is in him. Remember that

YOUR VOICE IS BEST FOR YOU.

It will serve every use, with due care and training, that you as a speaker will ever have for it. Only rarely are there physical defects or pathological conditions, and for these a physician should be consulted. A naturally weak or displeasing voice requires more training, that is all. Where one has "the Yankee habit of talking through the nose," which is really due to failing to talk through the nose, a wise vocalist can correct it.

It is not the voice, but the proper use of it, that brings success. Half the battle of delivery lies there. There are men on the platform speaking almost daily the year around to audiences of thousands, whom it is torture to hear. You fear every moment that they may give out. Would it not be worth the time and patience for them to have found their natural register, and learned how to breathe? For shallow breathing is often at the root of the trouble. Nature made the diaphragm as the bellows for the lungs. When it is drawn down, the air rushes in; when it is raised, the air is forced out. To learn whether you are breathing properly, lie on your back, and breathe naturally: in that position deep breaths are taken. Then stand up and breathe exactly as you did when lying down. Practice deep breathing before rising in the morning, by drawing in the breath gradually and slowly through the nose, holding it a moment, and then expelling it more rapidly through the open mouth. Breathe from the whole lung, both lower and upper. Not only will the above practice prove of value to the student as a lesson in proper breathing, but it is one of the cures recommended by neuropathists for nervousness. But it must not be carried to the point of fatigue, or dizziness. When the student has once learned how to use his voice properly, off the stage, its use in speaking becomes mechanical. I heard a local singer in the West complain to her audience that the basement hall in which we were gathered made it impossible for a singer to do credit to herself. The great prima donna, Emma Juch, happened to be in the city, and was invited to come to that basement and sing. No excuses were necessary on her part. Her divine voice flooded the room like a sea of heavenly melody.

Your voice, the one with which you were provided by nature, is best adapted to your physical constitution, and has all the quality and quantity necessary. A study of it will enable you to avoid its misuse, such as "glottic attack," "throaty tones," "head tones," "mouthing," and the rest. It demands no special training, as singing does. An ordinary voice, with proper enunciation, is all that is required. It takes less volume for the platform than it does to telephone. As you use your voice in private, you will use it in public. A hygienic method of life will do more for the voice than the best training, valuable as that is if one is to seek superior excellence. Without observing the rules of good health, training is thrown away. Your voice is born with your physical temperament, and will therefore be influenced by your physical condition. Prof. S. S. Curry: "So influential is the whole body over tone that bad breathing is often caused by bad poise. Hard, nasal tones are often caused by constriction of the body. . . . The body is much more vitally connected with the voice than the violin with its string and tone."

In case of sore throat, don't tamper with patent medicines as a remedy, though of course menthol or other cough drops may serve as a temporary palliative. Consult a competent physician. Wear a comfortable collar while speaking in public. Nathan Sheppard in his excellent *Before an Audience:* "If you awake in the night and find your mouth open, get up and close it." Don't be too self-conscious of your voice.

Begin in a moderate tone. This has three advantages: it enables the speaker to increase in volume as he proceeds; it gives him the poise of self-mastery; and it grips attention. Auditors have to listen when the speaker's voice is low, in order to hear what he is saying. Rhymes Dr. Leifchild:

> "Begin low,
> Go on slow;
> Rise higher,
> And take fire."

Use chest tones, but use them naturally. Speaking in the throat is a careless habit. It is distressing to listen to. It rasps the throat. As soon as a throaty speaker gets interested in what he is saying, his rasping tones begin just at that time when he is sure not to notice and correct them. Let him set a watch before the doors of his mouth in conversation, and in unimpassioned speech.

Open the mouth. Notice the mouths of good solo singers, and contrast them with volunteers in a country choir. A rotund expression cannot squeeze through half-shut doors without scraping off part of its beauty of form. A beginner fancies that "people will look at him" if he opens his mouth wide. The opposite is the case. It is the closed lips that make an auditor wonder what makes the speaker "make faces" with his mouth. Try to say:

"Oh, say, can you see by the dawn's early light,"

keeping your teeth together, and see how it sounds! It produces the impression of that old-time saint that used to say in the prayer-meeting: "I will lay my hand on my mouth, and my mouth in the dust, and cry, 'Unclean! unclean! God be merciful to me a sinner!'" After such a jumble of texts from various parts of the Bible, with the picture of a man trying to cry anything with his hand on his mouth and his mouth in the dust, one does not wonder at his plea for divine mercy: it is the only source from which he can expect any. Practice opening the mouth by shouting, *Obadiah,* which is said to be the sound that carries farthest. I would remind preachers of the promise of Jehovah: "I will give thee the opening of the mouth in the midst of them"; and, "Open thy mouth wide, and I will fill it."

I close this chapter with one of the most important precepts that can be given to the student of public speech: Practice continually. Use your voice every day, in every way, and it will get better and better. Sing. If you don't know how to sing, sing anyhow, in the great open spaces, far from censorious neighbors. Do not be over-fearful of wearing your voice out. If used naturally, it will grow ever stronger and more flexible by constant use, if not too long at a stretch. Stand on the seashore and sing against the rolling surf. Stand a long distance from your fellow student, and each shout to the other without screaming. Read something aloud every day, not only as practice in enunciation and inflection, but for the sake of strengthening your voice. The voice is built up by exercise, as the biceps are. Tiring of the "comedy parson, one of the standing jokes on the English variety stage," the Associate Press announced in 1924 that under the enthusiastic support of the Archbishops Canterbury and York, a scheme was launched, with an initial sum of two thousand pounds, whereby all theological students preparing for holy orders in the Church of England are to be trained in the right production and management of the voice. Teachers are to insure the public that clergymen will be taught to read and speak with "clearness, sympathy and reverence." Accept every opportunity for speaking in public. No books or lecture courses will begin to teach you as practice does. Books and extension courses are essential aids, and are indispensable preventives of false habits. But they have value only in carrying out in public what they teach in private.

Work over your voice determinedly. Its use will take a lifetime of thought and study to make it a vehicle that shall be worthy of its owner's expression. In learning to speak German and French, you were willing to spend a week of hard work to get the single sounds of the German *ich* and the French *ü*. Devote equal diligence to the lifetime task of perfecting the voice, the most divine musical instrument in all God's orchestra. Think of the time the Creator took to make your voice, and patience will play handmaid to your ambition, till your

> "poor, lisping, stammering tongue
> Lies silent in the grave."

The serious study of voice with an eye to its development requires persistent and extended effort, and will pay dividends in clarity of tone, resonance, carrying-power, and tone quality. The reader who wishes to improve his vocal apparatus will find several excellent guides listed in the Bibliography. He should purchase one, or borrow it from a library, and follow the program of voice culture outlined for him by the author of the handbook.

In capsule form, voice culture consists in the development of all the physical factors involved in the production of vocal tones:

a. Breathing should be deep, lung-filling, and under the con-

trol of the diaphragm. Draw deep breaths, and practice
sending the air out in short puffs driven from the diaphragm. Draw deeply and count as far as you can; seek
to lengthen the count as the days go by.

b. The throat must be relaxed. Practice slow rotation of the
head, feeling for muscle relaxation; try a long yawn to
loosen the muscles around the vocal chords.

c. The tongue must be flexible and active. Try running the
tip of the tongue around both sides of the teeth, from
the back at one side around to the back of the other, upper
and lower. Make a program of doing this regularly, while
doing manual labor or reading the evening paper. Try
the tongue twisters which depend upon the "s" sound.

d. The lips must be free and active. Try pouting them and
then rotating the pout. Practice the "tongue-twisters"
which depend on the sound of "p" like Peter Piper, or
"w" like How Much Wood. . . . Use the lips for projec-
tion, aiming your words like a steady stream of tracer
bullets at the opposite wall.

e. The mouth must open wide and freely. Practice making
the lower jaw "flap" as you shake your head from side to
side. Repeat words with the "ow" sound, like the familiar
"how, now, brown cow."

These relatively simple exercises will keep your voice in trim.
More serious study for improvement in resonance and quality
must be made from manuals devoted especially to vocal culture.

8

THE VOICE

Part 2

"It was a beautiful violin: the proportions were right, the curve of the neck and head was just what it should be, the color was dark and rich, and the polish such as only time and loving care can give.

" 'It looks like a genuine old Cremona,' said the connoisseur, 'but give me the bow.'

"He drew it once or twice across the strings, then laid it down, and the violin with it. 'No,' he said, 'it's only an ordinary fiddle. A real old Cremona always speaks with the voice of a gentleman. This talks like an auctioneer.' "

There are two things that mark the man—his voice and his stride. Even more definitely than of the physical man, does voice reveal character. That is one of those "mysterious" reasons why it has such a magic influence on the hearer.

The machinery for tone making is a masterpiece of ingenious construction. Tone is manufactured by the "double resonator," that is, the oral and nasal cavities. Both open from the pharynx, the chamber above the vocal chords, running back beyond the soft palate. Unnatural tones, the psychologist would say, are "made on purpose"; meaning that some false constraint or habit of rigidity is interfering with nature. To give nature her chance to produce rich and varied tones, relax the throat. Before the speaker can cooperate with nature, he must stop fighting her. If he will use his voice as naturally as children at play, he will be surprised with the result. His throat is made to be used.

Every tone must be a full tone. "A small tone is not part of a tone," as a child is not part of a human being, but a whole one in miniature. Says John Whitcomb Nash, famous basso:

"Vowels are the sound element, the tone vehicles: they carry the tone." Therefore, give the vowels their full significance. Variety of the voice is not a strangling or twisting of the tone; nor an elision or clipping of the tone; it is only a change in size or quality.

Various methods are suggested for finding the range and optimum pitch of the speaking voice. One is this: sit at the piano and hum with open mouth down the scale until you arrive at the note lowest in the scale which you can make clearly and without breaking. Strike this note and then hum up the scale four or five white keys. This point indicates the range of your optimum speaking pitch, from which your voice should rise and fall for inflection. Train yourself to speak both in conversation and from the platform with this basic pitch as your normal speaking voice.

One cannot too strongly urge variety in the use of the voice. Variety is simply an adaptation of tone to thought and feeling. Prof. Curry emphasizes this in *Vocal and Literary Interpretation of the Bible:* "The problem of improving vocal expression is peculiar. It cannot be developed by mechanical, artificial, or objective methods. Its unfolding requires a more vital process than that of written language. Its improvement requires primarily the stimulation and accentuation of the processes of thinking— the awakening of deeper feeling, and a higher realization of truth." A musician's feelings find more play on the strings of a violin than on a resined bit of twine fastened to the bottom of a tin can. Variety of tone is vital, if a speech is to be more than two minutes long. Monotony kills. The very word *monotony* means one tone. Monotony buries thought. The audience have to work harder than the speaker; and then they don't know whether they will be rewarded for it or not. With the exception of the Catholic Church, where the priest is the representative of the people, and takes their place in the function of worship, and therefore where droning in Latin is appropriate to the purpose of the service, the average audience goes to hear a speech they can most easily comprehend. Even when the speaker gives them what he has to say in perfect form, they carry away little enough of it. Therefore let him exert every effort to hand them all he can. Try droning the twenty-third Psalm, and listen to yourself doing it; and then see how you would like to have to hear it every time you speak.

Monotony leaves motives of action untouched. Instead of lighting the fires of the will, monotony closes off the channels by which the will is reached. The listener sets up resistance to the wearisome sameness of tone, and in so doing he sets up equal resistance to the message that tone is supposed to convey. Flee monotony. Use or purchase a tape recording machine so that you may hear yourself as others must; and if the deadly monotone is there, give yourself no rest until it has been conquered by liveliness, by deep feeling, by flexible intonation, all based upon the determination to touch human hearts with the truth in love.

Vary the pitch of your voice, in speaking in public. Intense and natural feeling will lead you to do this. But, if you haven't the feeling, then do it deliberately! If you are speaking in a high pitch, drop to low; if in low register, go up to high. The change this effects in the attitude of the audience will be argument enough; the change it makes in your own feelings, the sense of freshness and revivifying it brings will lead you to repeat it. When variety is deliberately adopted, care must be had not to make the change of pitch itself monotonous by periodic rise and fall. Monotonous variety is one of the most distressing forms of monotony. The reason an idea at times impresses one as something quite new, is because it has been presented in a new tone of voice. We like to hear Chinese chatter, because the language is built on tone and half-tone changes, so that the same sound has eight or ten different meanings according to the pitch of the voice. The same thing is true of preaching. Dr. Byram writes in the preface to Fordyce's *Art of Preaching:*

> "For, what's a sermon, good or bad.
> If a man reads it like a lad?
> To hear some people, when they preach,
> How they run o'er all parts of speech,
> And neither raise a word, nor sink;
> Our learned bishops, one would think,
> Had taken school-boys from the rod,
> To make 'embassadors of God.'"

American conversation is marked by its emphasis; English and

Continental, by their cadence. Each has its justification, each
its charm for the ear. I shall not discuss inflections, as their use
is self-evident. Too much instruction in matters of minute detail
tends to render the student self-conscious. It is, however, well
to remember in passing that the use of the falling slide at the
close of a sentence or a clause gives dignity to the thought. Read
with rising, and then with falling inflection these familiar lines
from the book of *Philippians:*

> "Finally, brethren, whatsoever things are true, whatsoever things
> are honorable, whatsoever things are just, whatsoever things are pure,
> whatsoever things are lovely, whatsoever things are of good report;
> if there be any virtue, and if there be any praise, think on these
> things."

Next, it is of consequence that there shall be variety in volume and the force with which one speaks. It must be borne in
mind that volume and force are by no means synonymous with
loudness. Loudness often defeats force and volume. Force is a
matter of intensity of feeling, rather than of shouting. Volume
demands the open throat, and full clear tone. Force is the conveyance of mental and emotional earnestness to the tone. A
giant, mentally and spiritually, may convey force by a whisper.
However, force and volume often require loud tones. Dr. John
Hall of New York had an effective way of bringing out occasionally a single word that he wished to emphasize, with a sudden
shout. It had the desired result of emphasis, and imparted a
clamant variety to his utterance. If he had shouted every sentence, as some old style Southern orators did, variety would have
been drowned and the audience would have wilted like Jonah
under the continuous blast of the East wind. As pitch is divided
into high, low and medium, so volume may be loud, soft, and
medium, the medium quality in both cases being the average
speaking tones required by the building and occasion. You are
to use more than voice enough to fill the room. To do this, while
it requires considerable experience, yet by glancing around the
room as you enter it, you can form a fairly accurate estimate
of the amount of voice needed. I heard a famous speaker ask
those in the rear gallery to hold up their hands if they could
hear him plainly, as he began to speak. It may be he did this
in order to establish a personal connection with those in the

distant gallery. Such tests are usually not necessary. The necessity for voice cultivation becomes evident when unusual conditions call for a volume far greater than an ordinary occasion would demand. When I was in college, I preached one Sunday morning in the second story of a building with a low ceiling, and a flat tin roof, in a terrific thunder storm. I was glad that I could match thunder with thunder and be heard without undue strain. The error of the inexperienced is in speaking too low. It is far better not to speak at all than to speak so as not to be heard. If a man wants to talk to himself, he doesn't need an audience to watch him. To overcome the rustling that is always going on in an audience, to contend with unsuspected poverty of acoustics, to make the deaf hear, these are the three reasons why you should use more voice than will just fill the house.

The idea sometimes advanced that principles should be practiced off the platform in private until they become automatic or mechanical, is true only to a limited degree. The essentials of speaking are in the long run learned only by practice before an audience. While one should become as familiar as possible with what he needs to do before he is called upon to do it, so that his attention can be devoted to what he is saying when he comes to say it, yet he can see how these laws work only while working. It is evident that this is true of the amount of volume necessary for a certain building. It must be increased by a conscious act of the will while the speaker is gauging the present need. To speak a little more loudly than will fill the house is to win the gratitude of your hearers. Yet it is equally true that you can use only what you have, and the volume of voice is a reservoir that is filled by constant practice—just as the mind is—when by one's self. Demosthenes learned much while speaking; he learned more while not speaking. Business and the business college together make the business man. Study the voices of successful speakers, and their manner of using them. A great speaker never makes it cumbrous to catch every word he is speaking. Yet he has his voice under perfect control. He does not speak loudly all the time. Shrieking, howling and roaring are torture to an audience. Continuous loud speaking leaves no chance for emphasis. Where everything is emphasized, nothing is.

Emphasis requires volume. Emphasis is essential to convey the meaning, and also to convey the feeling, of the speaker. Prof. D. E. Watkins states: "Emphasis is the same thing in a sentence that accent is in a word." Repeat with, and then without emphasis, these lines:

> "Strike for your altars and your fires!
> Strike till the last armed foe expires!"

Voice-volume is to be adapted to the purpose in hand. Most of your speech is to be delivered in the middle or narrative register; and from this as a base, stronger or milder tones ascend or descend, according to the thought. Just as a novel, proceeding in narrative form, departs on occasion now to animated and lively discourse, now to exciting adventure or pathetic scenes, the flexibility of a trained voice adjusts itself to its owner's demands, as he will. Some attacks call for the "whiz-bang," some for the "twenty-two." A change of volume does much to hold the attention of the hearer.

There must be variety also in the rate, or speed. There is a marked difference between speakers in their habitual rate of utterance. Phillips Brooks spoke with impetuous rapidity, his very speed deepening the impression of his earnestness. His enunciation was so clear that not a word was lost. One could not imagine Daniel Webster, however, speaking thus. Most beginners are too rapid. There are dull minds before them to whom, as one such complained, such a speaker is "a flash, and he sits down." He got nothing. The thought on important subjects should be too profound to run helter skelter across the field. Often the young speaker is proud to boast that he has "talked two hundred and fifty words a minute," instead of making a lasting impression on the thoughts or character of those that struggled to get what he was driving at. Clearness is sacrificed by too rapid talk. Swiftly running streams lose their transparency. True dignity is not in a hurry to get through. Impressiveness is sacrificed. A sense of levity is imparted. When one is hurried for time, he loses more than he gains by speaking rapidly. The wise thing, in such cases, is either to decline to speak, after others on the program have exhausted the hour, or else to leave out part of what you have prepared, for the sake of making effectual what is spoken. Never be in a hurry. A nervous haste destroys the influence of all you are doing. When President Taft was introduced, at the last moment, to the Yale Club of Southern California, he spoke quietly for twenty minutes, though a great banquet of the city's most eminent citizens was impatiently waiting in the next room. The fact that dinner was getting cold at twenty-five dollars a plate, and that his supporters were champing their bits, did not ruffle his imperturbable good humor, nor rob him of the dignity of worthy utterance.

One of the most profitable devices in connection with the question of rate is the pause. Rapid speakers generally omit it altogether. Beginners are slow to learn its remarkable effectiveness. It must follow an important thought, or the central word, to let it sink in, in its full significance; or a pause must precede them. When a transition is reached, and one begins the next division of the discourse, unless there is a distinct pause there will be a jumble of ideas resulting in confusion. The effect a pause produces on an audience is a revelation to the student, when he uses it for the first time. Inattention, rustle, drowsiness, instantly cease, all eyes turn toward the platform. Silence captures your audience, as noise can never do. The question is raised by every mind: "What is coming?" and then immediately after: "What has just been said?" The value of attention in the presentation of a profound thought, or of a witty one, is recognized. Who was it: "He is eloquent, whether he is speaking or not"? The pause serves much the same purpose as a tree in the foreground of a photograph, by adding charm through partial concealment. Pauses refresh an audience, like the rest in music. In aiming to speak more slowly, it is frequently necessary only to lengthen your pauses. Do not let the pause last too long. Too long a pause gives the impression of a break, as if the speaker had forgotten, or were dawdling. A pause is like ornament: it is introduced for the purpose of attracting attention to the subject, not to itself.

In enthusiasm, or in excitement, and in some types of humor, the rate is rapid. A sudden burst of speed, like an express passing a slow freight, affords variety, and requires attention on the listener's part. Try drawling the lines:

"Hew down the bridge, Sir Consul,
   With all the speed ye may;
I with two more to help me
   Will hold the foe in play."

A sentence, begun in a moderate tone, may grow rapid as it proceeds, keeping pace with the rising fires within. The fiery Bob Shuler of Los Angeles in a Prohibition campaign: "They say, let the minister leave politics alone, and go back to the pulpit. I'm not going to *stand by and see my country go to ruin!*" Vary the speed constantly, for the sake of the audience.

Vary the quality of tone to suit the word, in onomatopoeia, the adaptation of sound to sense, through vocal imitation, in words like *ring, roar, bells, hiss, crash,* etc. These words themselves interpret their vocalization. Vary also to suit the occasion. A set oration on a date of national significance, like Armistice Day, or the Fourth of July, will naturally take, as it proceeds, the "orotund" or grand tone; a religious, the dignified quality; a funeral sermon, tender quality. This is in harmony with what has been said about the conversational voice for speaking in public. Each of these tones will be employed in conversation, if the corresponding sentiments be felt. The tone must be varied to suit the thought. Esenwein has given four illustrations:

> *Pure tone:* "Listen, my children, and you shall hear of the midnight ride of Paul Revere."
> *Orotund:* "Roll on, thou deep and dark blue ocean, roll!"
> *Aspirate:* "Hush! sure, you heard it then!"
> *Guttural:* "Let the carrion rot!"

Humor, often best expressed by sprightly tones, is sometimes more effectively expressed by assuming a monotonous, or even melancholy, drawl. Mark Twain's solemn drawl was irresistible: "Education is everything. The peach was once a bitter almond; cauliflower is nothing but cabbage with a college education." So was Bob Burdette's cheerful whine: "Children are not educated at school; they are educated at their mother's knee—or across it." Pathos sinks to bathos, unless it is expressed in tender tone. A gigantic clergyman in the West told me that it was impossible for him to modulate the ferocity of his harsh voice; and that it had often proved embarrassing to him in conducting funeral services to roar his consolation with the bellow of a bull of Bashan.

Running description adopts the narrative tone. Passion, blazing in the soul, sets fire to the voice. Argument, as in a debate, takes the logical tone. Anger and joy are expressed just as they are in conversation. In an appeal to the heart, as in a Memorial Day address, or at the close of a sermon, even though the volume be loud, the tone is gentle, and deeply sympathetic. Two cautions are however here necessary. Never let the voice drop to a whisper. When a speaker who has cultivated the habit of whispering thinks he is being impressive, he is only making his audience mad at him. A similar execrable habit is that of letting the voice drop at the close of a sentence, and thus rendering the most important part of the sentence inaudible to the hearers.

Seek not great things for yourself; but as an expert mighty man in the hour of the concussion of spirits, throw your whole soul into the training of your voice. It will richly repay all the toil you may put upon it. Build a breadth of mind, a depth of feeling that will bring a newborn tone-color to your vocal production. Then you will kindle a fire by the grace of God that shall never go out.

> "If I were a voice, a persuasive voice,
>   That could travel the wide world through,
> I would fly on the beams of the morning light,
> And speak to men with a gentle might,
>   And tell them to be true.
> I would fly, I would fly over land and sea,
> Wherever a human heart might be,
> Telling a tale, or singing a song,
> In praise of the right, in blame of the wrong.
>
> "If I were a voice, a consoling voice,
>   I'd fly on the wings of the air;
> The homes of sorrow and guilt I'd seek
> And calm and truthful words I'd speak,
>   To save them from despair.
> I would fly, I would fly o'er a crowded town,
> And drop like the happy sunlight down
> Into the hearts of suffering men,
> And teach them to look up again.
>
> "If I were a voice, a convincing voice,
>   I'd travel with the wind;

And wherever I saw the nations torn
By warfare, jealousy, spite or scorn,
        Or hatred of their kind,
I would fly, I would fly on the thunder crash,
And into their blinded bosoms flash;
Then, with their evil thoughts subdued,
I'd teach them Christian brotherhood.

"If I were a voice, an immortal voice,
        I would fly the earth around;
And wherever man to his idols bowed
I'd publish in notes both long and loud
        The gospel's joyful sound.
I would fly, I would fly on the wings of day,
Proclaiming peace on my world-wide way,
Bidding the saddened earth rejoice."

9

THE "HOLY TONE"

After what I have written about the necessity of adapting the voice to the idea to be expressed, I want to utter a warning against a common form of adaptation which is artificial. A foghorn is monotonous, but it is a genuine adaptation to its purpose. Many addresses, perhaps sermons more than others, are rendered useless by the unnatural tone in which they are delivered. The most noticeable effect is that they are apparently doubled in length when spoken in this sanctified singsong. Said Sydney Smith, the witty English preacher: "Some men preach as if they thought sin is to be taken out of a man as Eve was taken out of Adam, by casting him into a profound slumber." It might be said of such churches, as it is of Westminster Abbey: "Many persons sleep within these walls."

The preacher feels the solemnity of the occasion. The pulpit is elevated above the congregation; the subject matter discussed is sublimated; the surroundings are churchly; the day is the Lord's Day. These facts seem to isolate him from daily life. The situation seems to him to demand a special tone of voice, in order to deepen the impression, and fit him into his environment. But it should never be forgotten that a false note cannot produce a true effect. A sense of unreality is produced. The bane of professionalism is substituted for the spirit of naturalness. There are six paramount objections to the use of the holy tone. (1) It sidetracks the attention; just as it is difficult to keep the mind on a monotonous book, or on a dull pain. (2) It stifles conviction, and thus actually defeats the very end for which it is assumed. (3) It wearies the hearer, instead of kindling his mind into alertness as an earnest address ought to do. (4) It withers the freshness of the Bible. Some one has said that the inspiration of the Bible is proved from the fact that it has outlived the defences of its friends. (5) It will reduce attendance at church. Pose is out of style. It is a melancholy sight to see speakers, who enjoy being listened to, taking effective means to keep listeners away. Isaiah warns people not "to seek unto them that chirp and that mutter." The obtuseness of speakers to what people want in a speech is a constant amazement to the teacher of public speaking. Yet speakers are no farther behind than members of other professions in a knowledge of what makes for success in their chosen calling. Most defeats are self-induced. (6) It has brought racy ridicule on the preacher, specially in Great Britain. He cannot prevail with it. Professional manner deceives only the simple. Artificiality is a psychological trap; and traps do not flatter the birds they are set to catch. Such ridicule is sometimes a means of grace. A pompous ministry has only itself to blame for the good-natured contempt in which it is sometimes held. Curry, from his experience with several divinity schools, claims to have discovered that "each denomination of Christians has something of a tone peculiar to itself. All these speech tones are faults of melody; they have their root in some variation of conversational form."

The holy tone is not a new defect, nor is it confined to the pulpit. It has given us the tremolo in singing. It is a blight on the legal, and other speaking professions. Julius Caesar asked a reader: "Do you read, or sing? If you sing, you sing very ill." The satirical Dean Swift, in an essay, *The Operation of the Spirit*:

> "Cant and droning supply the place of sense and reason in the language of men. The naturalists observe that there is in human noses an idiosyncrasy by virtue of which, the more the passage is obstructed, the more our speech delights to go through; as the music of a flageolet is made by the stops. . . . In a short time, no doctrine passed for sound and orthodox, unless it were delivered through the nose. Strait, every pastor copied after this original."

Such sound doctrine makes sound sleepers. It is like that soft stage music which Fielding said was played during love scenes, "either to soothe the audience with the softness of the tender passion, or to lull and prepare them for that gentle slumber in which they will most probably be composed by the ensuing scene." Is there any torture greater than that of struggling to keep awake in church? I quote these authors of preceding centuries that their wholesome ridicule may show how ancient is this vocal curse. Artificial tones have no excuse. The manly Dean of St. Patrick's again: "Opium is not so stupefying to many persons as an afternoon sermon. . . . That it is the very sound of the sermon which bindeth up their faculties is manifest from hence, because they all awake so very regularly as soon as it ceaseth, and with much devotion receive the blessing."

There is an individual slant, a personal pitch, to the voice of these parrot-talkers. The holy tone varies with the speaker. No two trees in the forest catch the breezes of heaven alike. No two mature bullfrogs croak on the same key. No two sets of human vocal cords vibrate on the same level. One is an unrelieving monotone, whose army of words marches in platoons, like cadets on parade; instead of thundering into the hearts, like a modern Boanerges. There is a rising inflection at the end. If Mark Antony had been in a professional state of mind at the funeral of Caesar, he would have spoken as follows—until the stones of Rome cried out in mutiny:

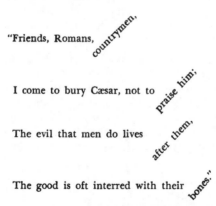

"Friends, Romans, countrymen,

I come to bury Cæsar, not to praise him;

The evil that men do lives after them,

The good is oft interred with their bones."

Others roll their sentences up a slope, like Sisyphus in Dante's hell, only to have them roll down again. They rise and fall like sheep going over a fence.

"The king of France and his ten thousand men
Marched up the hill, and then marched down again."

Variety of tone is essential and commendable when it has a purpose; but it is torture when it has no purpose. There is such a thing as an unvarying variety. Richard Steele, who suffered many things of many speakers, dubbed these mechanical variationists "Pindaric":

"There is one sort of person in the pulpit I call Pindaric readers, as confined to no one set measure: these pronounce five or six words with great deliberation, and the five or six subsequent ones with as great celerity; the first part of a sentence with a very exalted voice, and the last part with a submissive one; sometimes again with one sort of tone, and immediately afterward with a very different one."

A natural tone brings warmth and light, like the sunshine; bombast is like a Northwest gale, breaking down every growing blossom in its path. Wrote Emerson: "The sweetest music is not the oratorio, but the human voice, speaking forth from its instant life tones of truth, tenderness, and courage." When the Psalmist praises the Creator for "the stormy wind, fulfilling his word," he limits it to inanimate nature. Only the devil goeth about as a roaring lion, seeking whom he may devour. Elijah found that God was not in the thunder nor in the earthquake, but in the still small voice.

What is the cause for the holy tone? It is not far to seek, nor difficult to remedy. If it were as hard to cure as it is contagious and deadening in its influence, more study would have been spent on it, and more effort taken to overcome it. With old men, it is maintained by the momentum of habit, a "stale fervor." In periods of rapt enthusiasm, as in a political campaign or a moral upheaval, words pour out hot, like streams of molten lava. As Keats:

"Words that have drawn transcendent meanings up
From the best passion of all bygone time;
By repetition waned to vexing wind."

The speaker's passion having cooled, he hopes his tone will conceal the change that has come over his emotion. And so this "falsetto whine" becomes chronic, like a neglected rheumatism.

The hope, however, that the old tones will produce the old effect is a delusion. The lips will obey the heart. A man's manner shows him to the audience for what he is, not for what he hopes they will think him to be. The impression he produces on candid minds is that he has lost faith in his message.

Rant is the child of cant. Cant is the monument we raise over the grave of a dead experience. A defunct enthusiasm cannot, like a frog, be made to leap again by the application of a galvanic current. Almost everything can be successfully imitated, except life. The reader will enjoy the old definition of cant, I think from the pen of Dean Swift: "Cant is by some people derived from one Andrew Cant, who they say was a Presbyterian minister from some illiterate part of Scotland, who by exercise and use had obtained the faculty, alias gift, of talking in the pulpit in such a dialect that it was said he was understood by none but his congregation, and not by all of them."

With young speakers, this "turgid jargon in mouthfilling rodomontade" arises by imitation or, more accurately, from fear of the audience. This fear they attempt to overcome not by love, which is the only way the fear of men can be vanquished, but by a false self-elevation that shall raise them above their fellows. Just as many social aspirants, on entering society, try to hide their weakness from the eyes of criticism by wearing expensive jewelry, a high hat, spats, or a cane. It is an attempt to lengthen a limited personality. Limitation begets imitation; imitation begets limitation. An auctioneer's tone is made unnatural by selling second-hand goods.

The cure for the holy tone is surprisingly simple: cease ranting or whining, and go to talking. "No one ever thinks or feels monotonously." Stop short, wait a minute, and then go on in a conversational tone of voice. You will be amazed at the effect this will have on the audience. They will revive like June flowers after a summer rain. It has been the conviction of the unnatural tonist that natural accents will make an audience indifferent to what he is saying. "They hear such tones everywhere, on the street, in the schoolroom, at the dinner table; they will become indifferent when they hear them; a sublimated tone will bring sublimated attention." The exact opposite is the case: an unnatural tone creates an indifference to the speech that is being

made, and disgust for the speaker that is making it. Try it and
see!

The minister has the advantage of a large and often vacant
auditorium in which to practice not only his speech but also
reading aloud. Handbooks to voice culture will provide numerous selections designed to develop various vocal qualities, and
to overcome the "holy tone" and other forms of monotony. These
should be read aloud in the empty auditorium, though the reader
must imagine that the room is filled with listeners. Select poetry
and prose on your own for such practice. Vary your reading; and
if you have a recording machine, be sure to use it frequently.

Phonograph recordings by distinguished readers, often by the
famous poets reading their own lines, are available. Compare the
recording of your own reading of a poem by, say, Robert Frost
with his reading of it as provided by the several recordings he has
made; and so on. Learn to listen for vocal variety, and then listen
to yourself. The "holy tone" and like forms of monotony can be
cured if the speaker learns to hear them in himself, and will give
the time and devotion to doing better.

10

MANNER AND MANNERISMS

Every speech is a lottery. A moment before beginning, you know no more as to the success of that speech than you know, when addressing a golf ball, where it is going to land. Yet success or failure is largely in the speaker's hands. He is master of his delivery; and on his delivery hangs, in large measure, the power of his address. Kate Douglas Wiggin, in *The Birds' Christmas Carol* says: "I wish I could get it into your heads that it ain't so much what you say as the way you say it." Delivery is at least only second to thought.

Almost every speaker's influence is neutralized, to some degree, by meaningless mannerisms that set the hearer's teeth on edge. An odd habit may cling to a speaker for years before he becomes conscious of it.

> "O, wad some power the giftie gie us
> To see oursels as others see us!
> It wad frae monie a blunder free us,
>   And foolish notion;
> What airs in dress and gait wad lae'e us,
> And e'en devotion."

"There are ridiculous traits in every one that all eyes see but his own." It might be more profitable for a student to collect mannerisms than butterflies. He could sometimes tabulate three from the same man. When scientifically spread out and tacked up, they would surpass for variety and color any other form of fungi.

A speaker is always in danger of acquiring new ones. With apologies to Bunyan:

> The orator is ever ill at ease:
> When one fault's gone, another doth him seize.

77

A mannerism becomes a habit. A speaking habit, like a riding-habit, fits close. Says Josh Billings: "Once get a man started down hill, and all nature seems greased for the occasion." A famous New England divine has the habit of closing his eyes now and then, and clasps his hands in a fatuous manner—a lady in the congregation calls it the "wicker-basket design." Another would hold down his thumb across his palm in gesturing, until one longed to pull it out. Another, in the West, thrusts his hand in his coat á la Napoleon at St. Helena. What makes them do it? Sometimes vanity, the instinctive "complex" of attracting attention to their bodily appearance. Sometimes it arises from embarrassment, as a child will twist at something; sometimes from too great a freedom from embarrassment. The speaker wants some use for his hands, and so nervously runs them through his hair, like Joseph Choate; another pulls his nose, or his ears, which are already quite long enough; another stands with arms a-kimbo like a New York washer woman; another plays with something on his desk, or twists a button—I have often wondered what would happen to his argument if that button came off! From an English essay, published 1792:

> "We are commonly enough disgusted by public speakers lisping and stammering, and speaking through the nose, and pronouncing the letter R through the throat, instead of the tongue, and the letter S like Th, and screaming above, or croaking below all natural pitch of human voice; some mumbling, as if they were conjuring up spirits; others bawling, as loud as the vociferous venders of provisions in London streets; some tumbling out the words so precipitately, that no ear can catch them; others dragging them out so slowly, that it is as tedious to listen to them as to count a great clock; some have got a habit of shrugging up the shoulders; others of see-sawing with their bodies, some backward and forward, others from side to side; some raise their eyebrows at every third word; some open their mouths frightfully; others keep their teeth so close together, that one would think their jaws were set; some shrivel all their features together into the middle of their faces; some push out their lips, as if they were mocking their audience; others hem at every pause; and others smack with their lips, and roll their tongue about in their mouths, as if they labored under a continual thirst. . . . They often ramble about with their eyes in a very unmeaning and unnatural manner."

If one must do something besides what he is there to do, let him acquire habits that won't prove so fascinating to his audience.

Let him take hold, though not in a desperate manner, of the corner of his desk. The Greeks, who are an impulsive, restless nation, have hit upon an ingenious device for occupying their hands. When I saw one of them in Athens leaning out of a car window and fingering a string of beads, I thought he was giving undue publicity to his rosary; but these are "Conversation beads," carried purposely as something to handle and thus let off his extra latinism.

Ask a relative or wise friend what your mannerisms are. If he hurts, he hurts to heal. "Depend upon it, if you are sensitive, self is very high up." The man that is not willing to acknowledge his faults is a coward. To acknowledge them, you must first see them, and this you can do in this instance only through another's eye. A professional critic is not needed; a wife knows more about her husband's platform excellences and defects than either he or his professor; she sees them oftener and loves him better. No man knoweth his own mannerisms. If he shrinks from criticism, let him go on making a fool of himself. Beware of flattery, and never let even well-meant praise close your ears to criticism and suggestion. There is no future for the speaker that cannot take advice. He that being often reproved hardeneth his neck, shall suddenly be destroyed and that without remedy. Don't defend yourself. Your enemies may render you a service for which you will never cease to be thankful. Your critic is your friend. Was it Beecher who said: "He that does not learn from his own mistakes turns the best schoolmaster out of his life"?

Use your will against your weaknesses. Will finds a way. Facing an obstacle, it climbs over it; if it cannot climb over, it tunnels under; if it cannot tunnel under, it goes around; if it cannot climb over, or tunnel under, or go around the obstacle, it flies at it, and the obstacle gives way.

Let your manner be natural and unconstrained. Don't count on being brilliant. We grow by absorbing the thought and manners of our superiors, all of us being unconscious plagiarists. There has been a deal of controversial talk in manuals of elocution and public speaking about "being natural," it being explained that for a beginner to be "natural" is to be uncouth and awkward, for these are natural to him at that stage; and that real naturalness is the result only of the highest art. While this is

all true, yet everybody knows what we mean by "being natural."
Our attitude to our audience is to be wholesome and free from
self-consciousness.

To be natural, the spirit must be natural. The difference between a crystal and an organism is that the crystal grows from
external accretions, and the organism grows from within. The
one is built, the other a builder. Shakespeare's advice in *Hamlet*
has become a classic: "Oh, there be players that I have seen play
—and heard others praise, and that highly—not to speak it pro-
fanely, that, neither having the accent of Christians, nor the gait
of Christian, pagan, or man, have so strutted and bellowed that
I have thought some of Nature's journeymen had made men and
not made them well, they imitated humanity so abominably."
Get the right frame of mind before speaking.

By sympathy with the audience, naturalness of manner comes.
Ask yourself, "How do *I* feel when I am in the audience?" You
will then recall that there is a stiffness and constraint when one
is surrounded by strangers and waiting for things to begin. Perhaps the hearer has been prejudiced against your point of view
by the inconsistencies or one-sided theories of persons he has met
or has lived with. Get the point of view of the various types of
hearers named in a previous chapter.

A natural manner is cultivated by constant contact with people.
Spend time in conversation with all classes. A writer describing,
I think, two bitter enemies shut by storm in the same cabin for
several days, makes the general observation that there are few
persons on the surface of the earth from whom, after an association of several days, we should not part with regret. No one can
feel at home in the presence of the unknown. Often men have
been compared to books. Who can know or love a book by seeing
its cover only? I used to think that men who spent a good deal
of time talking with others were idlers. One wonders at the pro-
motion of unknown rustics from obscure villages; but they were
"perusing mankind in th' original" in those political debates
that waxed so hot on the upturned kegs and boxes around the
country stove, in the "general" store. Traveling is of inestimable
value to the student of public speaking, giving him as it does a
knowledge of the way the world thinks and acts. Webster wrote
to Charles Sumner: "Converse, *converse*, CONVERSE, with living

men, face to face, and mind to mind—that is one of the best sources of knowledge."

Train the body to become lithe, easy and graceful, till grace becomes an instinct, as it does in an animal. It is a delight to watch the movements of some speakers. Golf, tennis, skating, some form of light outdoor manual labor, and home dancing, are valuable aids to good physical form and grace of movement.

Cultivate freedom. Just as in a dentist's chair it hurts less when you relax and "let go," so all the dread specters that gather about the beginner's platform, and occasionally in later years and in unexpected circumstances, will fold their tents like the Arabs and silently steal away, if you shake them off, and "make yourself at home." Forget them. Say to yourself, "I am going to have a good time, and will see that my audience does." A personal illustration will be pardoned, as it is apropos of the situation of thousands. It was at the great summer assembly at Martha's Vineyard. I was on for a twenty minutes' speech, one of the first I ever delivered, being still in college. All native New Englanders will know how I felt, bound hand and foot by reserve, bashfulness, and self-consciousness. I needed all the help of God and man, both of whom seemed far away. Bloody battles on athletic fields, and a tremendous enthusiasm for my subject, put me through. I found that these two things are not enough to make a public speaker. I spoke with great rapidity, condensing into twenty minutes enough material, if suitably amplified, to have covered two hours; neither raised nor lowered my voice; nor stirred hand or foot. When I came down from the platform, Dr. E. P. Parker, the well-known Hartford pastor, drew me to a chair beside him, and gave me a bit of advice I shall profit by as long as I live: "Young man, what you need is what the French call *abandon.*" What a luminous word! Emancipation. As one of my students, a big country lad, recently put it in an examination, "to cut loose." If it is constitutional to you to be conventional, rise above your constitution. In my own case, the heat of battle has sometimes borne me a trifle too far, to the peril of tall platform lamp-stands, or other furniture; but the old stiff constraint fled at Dr. Parker's command, never to return. I hope this paragraph may do as much for some other captive. Catch Whittier's spirit:

"Hurrah! hurrah! the west wind comes freshening down the bay!
The rising sails are filling, give way, my lads, give way!"

An audience will forgive much in a speaker, just as we forgive
a baby everything, and for the same reason: because he is free
from entangling alliances, and master of himself and of his environment. Abandon is not a struggle, but a state. Lowell said:
"To seek to be natural, implies a consciousness that forbids all
naturalness forever." A word of self-command before leaving the
wings for the stage will make you master of your fate. Do not
strive for self-mastery, for freedom; just let go, as one does when
he *falls* in love. Be free. When Patrick Henry cried: "Give me
liberty, or give me death!" he knew that he would have to choose
one or the other. Be free. Emerson: "It is the vice of our public
speaking that it has not abandonment. Somewhere not only every
orator, but every man, should let out all the length of all the
lines." Adapt your manner to your thought, and to your audience. Esenwein writes on *Facing the Audience:* "Does the
thought require the familiarity of colloquial expression, the
directness of appeal, the dignity of elevated mood, or the fervor of
passion? Then rely upon the will in delivery." Some audiences
require a different manner on the platform from others. Occasions, and the speaker's moods, also differ. Consistency would
be a curse in a speaker. If there are paragraphs of advice in this
series that contradict other paragraphs, follow them both; just
as Presbyterians believe in both divine foreordination and human
free will; or as Congress emphasizes both nationalism and internationalism. The charm of public speaking is one that is always
learning to make readjustments. If pursuit be a greater joy than
attainment, he may be happy; for his pursuit for success is renewed at every public appearance. All that you learned when
you addressed that university audience in your baccalaureate
address has to be forgotten and an entirely new set of manners
adopted when you face a crowd of newsboys. The wrench you
get should serve to keep you broad awake. One day you speak
at a revival meeting in a movie theater, and the next day you talk
to a woman's club in their parlors. Platform manners must be
far more adjustable than table manners.

Let your manner never stoop to the cheap or vulgar. Maintain on every appearance your high level of men of culture,

refinement and purity of soul. The man that tells an unseemly anecdote at a men's smoker puts himself below the swine, that wallow only in the mire. Exhibit true dignity, even in an after-dinner talk. Lion cubs at play, or young eaglets, are never false to their kingly standards. Henry Drummond said, "It is surprising what an effect dignity has, especially on the undignified." An associate of men, Mr. George A. Warburton, General Secretary of the Young Men's Christian Association at Toronto wrote the following:

"Play the man!
With your *body*. Keep it fit
By the highest use of it.
For the service of the soul,
Every part in full control,
Strong for labor, deft to do
All that is required of you—
Play the man!

Play the man!
With your *mental* powers free
From all narrow bigotry;
Search for truth that it may bless
All your days with happiness.
Thus may brain and brawn agree,
Make you what you ought to be—
Play the man!

Play the man!
Keep your inmost *soul* as pure
As your mother's virtue. Sure
If within no evil dwells
There's no power in all the hells
Strong enough to drag you down,
Rob you of your manhood's crown—
Play the man!"

11

PLATFORM MAGNETISM

In connection with the memorial to our great American president, *The Literary Digest:* "To touch Theodore Roosevelt was to receive a spark, as from a live battery. No one ever came into close contact with him, in any of his countless activities, without feeling the stirring influence of his electric personality." There is a baffling charm about certain individuals that draws us like a magnet. In social circles they are the "life of the company." In business they are fascinating. On the platform, they are irresistible. Their example is contagious, their conversation bewitching.

A magnetic temperament gives its possessor easy superiority. A traveling salesman with this gift sells goods to merchants who are afterwards astonished that they have been charmed into buying what they did not want. It constitutes three-quarters of the attraction of many taking addresses. To the after-dinner speaker, as to the auctioneer, it is an indispensable asset. Ministers with this magic wand sway crowded houses, winning thousands of members. Read the reports of their sermons in the morning paper, and you will sometimes exclaim: "Why, he didn't say anything!" That is it: he said nothing, magnificently. The speaker with personal magnetism triumphs over all competitors. "The voice with the smile wins." A speaker is like the professional hypnotist who, with his suggestion conveys also his personality. Emerson believed that people read anecdotes of eloquence with an interest comparable only to the accounts of a famous battle. Such speakers are platform miracles.

This uncanny gift is not easy to define. Considering its magic powers, astonishingly little has been written about it. Works on efficiency, that are now flooding the bookstalls, ignore its existence. Psychology has not analysed it. What is this thing? It is as independent of the familiar laws of human influence as it is superior to them. Mental intelligence, physical perfection of face and form, exalted social station, may one or all be lacking to its fortunate possessor. The gods have seen fit to breathe upon him, that is all. What more need he ask? And it is a strange fact that people with personal magnetism often lack platform magnetism; and persons with platform magnetism often lose all their fascination as soon as they leave the platform.

Asked to name individuals with or without this gift, we can all do so instantly; asked to define it, the tongue halts. But we recognize it, and its possessor. When we associate with him, he fascinates us. When we see him in the distance, we smile with pleasure. When we think of him, our hearts thrill. If we were jurymen, and he on trial, or the lawyer for the defence, it would be battling against nature to convict him. Many an acquittal of filthy villains, incomprehensible to readers outside the court-room, is to be laid to the weird spell of an unprincipled attorney's magnetism. A recent juryman: "Yes, she would have been hanged, but she smiled, and we decided on a prison sentence." Some lawyers are so dull that they even make the gallows yawn. Let platform magnetism defend a Christian cause, and victory is assured beforehand.

Platform magnetism makes its possessor the "vogue." Nathan Sheppard: "An impression is produced by the speaker quite apart from and often in spite of the words he utters. It is a mesmeric influence, it is feeling, reflection, thought produced by the animal galvanic battery on two legs. An influence goes out of the speaker into the hearer. Something went out of Bonaparte into his soldiers; so his soldiers said. Doubtless the great warrior was a great animal galvanic battery on two legs, or six legs, counting the horse's." Labor follows the lead of the human magneto. The mystery that attended Abraham Lincoln's first nomination to the presidency is solved largely by the fact that he magneted his acquaintances. If he took his seat in a hotel lobby, and began to talk as he always did, the room filled to the doors and window-sills. Lloyd George is a veritable lodestone. When Bryan, in the face of science, denounced evolution, it was found necessary to call a convention of America's leading scientists to withstand his influence. Charlie Chaplin is said to care nothing for children; yet they would follow him to the world's edge. It was interesting to accompany Booker T. Washington into an exclusive woman's club and observe how the distance that was held between him and that aristocratic circle at his first appearance, narrowed to intimate social contact in the reception that followed the great negro's lecture. When "Billy" Sunday was on the platform, or Douglas Fairbanks on the screen, or Will Rogers was making a speech as former mayor of Beverly Hills, you could almost hear the "magnetic tick" in the breast of the audience. A friend of mine said to me that he would go a hundred miles to hear Mr. ——— preach; the man was not a great preacher; but those possessed with the magnetic sense can feel the pull when coming within the zone of radio-activity of some fulminating personality.

Has the discovery of the electron some secret of personality yet to be divulged? I have often wondered whether the magnetism of physics and the magnetism of psychology may not prove to be the same force. Are they identical? Magnetism is a recognized force in nature, about which science as yet knows little; does it exist in the human body? Here is an almost unexplored field for investigation. As early as November, 1923, Prof. George T. Fielding of the General Electric Company entered upon experiments with electric eels, in an attempt to verify his theory that the brain is an electric battery, supplying voltage energy to mind and motor nerve.

Or, is platform "magnetism" merely a figure of speech illustrating natural force in the mental world? The three best known authors in this field, Argyle in *Reign of Law,* Butler in the *Analogy,* and Drummond in *Natural Law in the Spiritual World,* three standard old-timers, do not refer to it. Lowell believed that the poet Dryden was the first to use the word in its metaphorical sense. The word *magnet* is from Magnesia, a district in Thessaly, where was found a metal that "looked like silver."

What are the sources of platform magnetism? Can it be acquired, in any degree, if the speaker be not one of those initially endowed at birth? It contains four salient elements. First, there is unquestionably the physical basis. Bodily condition is of paramount importance in the composition of a magnetic temperament. Vitality is contagious. Exuberance of spirits is accompanied, as everyone knows, by electric phenomena. The hair will not lie down. The fingers give out a spark, a shock. Whether the aroma of personality has an electro-magnetic source, that may be transmitted by magnetic therapy, we do not yet know. It will be rendering a valuable service to humanity for science to find out. That health is contagious, no less than disease, there is no doubt, at least so far as physical exhilaration can kindle enthusiastic response. The brain is a physical organ. As a tool of the mind, a good circulation sharpens it by physical friction. A "sanguine" temperament is not a mere figure of speech. Take deep breaths, remember that yours is a *community chest*. Dr. I. N. Clark of Kansas City had a bombshell gesture that acted upon his audiences like a charge of electricity. Health promotes competence in the speaker. He that would exercise his gifts must exercise his body.

The second ingredient of platform magnetism is humor. One would go far to find a winning character without it. He that would stir men magnetically must avail himself of it. Writes Bertrand Lyon: "Psychologists tell us that only ten per cent of an average audience will respond to an appeal of pure reason, only seventy per cent to an inspirational appeal, while over ninety per cent will respond instantly to humor." Go over in your mind the list of magnetical speakers you have been thinking of while reading this chapter, and try to name one wanting in this gift. It is the effervescence of life's cup. Its language is more nearly universal even than that of music. We condone the cynic, we cultivate the companionship of the dyspeptic, if they can laugh with us. Through laughter Lincoln won the nation, and endured the dark hours of the rebellion. "Billy" Sunday: "God loves fun; that's why he made the monkey, and the donkey, and some of you people." This was the source of the extraordinary magnetic power of Mark Twain, Robert J. Burdette, J. Whitcomb Riley. The wise speechwright will not ignore this source of power. Many a preacher, though he use it but sparingly in the pulpit, has been taught by observation that laughter may be the open door to the heart. Never laughter for laughter's sake. Wrote the poet Cowper:

" 'Tis pitiful to court a grin
When you would win a soul."

But laughter for the gospel's sake, as said Dr. J. W. Brougher,
for many years California's most popular pastor: "Years ago I
resolved to devote my sense of humor to the uplift of humanity.
I have had to fight for the privilege of doing it." Cheer often
disarms criticism. A merry countenance drieth up a back-biting
tongue. If as the Arabs say, "All sunshine makes the desert," it
is also true that gloomy clouds make the poisonous marsh. An
audience are like Indians; they ask, as the Rhode Island savages
did of Roger Williams, "What cheer?"

The third constituent of platform magnetism is enthusiasm.
It is not so much what you say, as the spirit with which you
say it, that finds favor with your audience. "People will run
to a fire" was a maxim, I think, of President Strong of Rochester.
An audience will cheer the man that is tremendously in earnest,
even though he have scarcely any other platform gift. Heat is
radiant. The earnestness of a speaker is often the only thing
that the hearers carry away. It is easier to start a fire than to
stop it. There is, in a blazing passion, a bewitching fascination
that captivates an audience. It acts like the "magnetic separa-
tion" of the physicist, drawing men from their environment,
as the Star in the East drew the group of wise men. "Nothing
but the fire kindles fire." "How is it that your Whitefield has
set the world on fire?" "Because he is on fire himself," answered
the great orator's friend. Theodore Roosevelt turned the big
stick into a firebrand. Popularity follows eagerness of spirit.
The "magnetic memory" of Thermopylae, Balaklava, Ypres, Iwo
Jima stirs the pulse, ignoring time and space.

"No accent of the Holy Ghost
This heedless world hath ever lost."

Half-heartedness is fatal to public influence. I would rather be
a fanatic than an icicle. All that is best in our national life is
owing to the magnetic retentivity of hearers that have been stirred
by the energy of great leaders, leaders that were large enough
to put the cause before the man.

But the reigning factor of platform magnetism, its crown, is
sympathy. Nothing wins like unselfish interest in others. The

magical charm of certain men, which can be resisted when they are absent, but to which all submit when they are present, lies in their keen interest in other human beings. They exert power over the heart because the heart is so well known to them. The hopes and fears of men, their loves and hates, are their lifelong study. Their knowledge has been gained more from social contact than from books. A young girl was so homely of face that she never received an invitation to the social gatherings of the young persons of her age. In her desperate loneliness, she said to herself: "Though I can never be popular like other girls, I will try to promote the happiness of others, by looking for opportunities to serve them." In time, she became the most popular girl of her circle. If we have not a pleasing personality, we can serve. That is the key to magnetism. We speak of the mysterious reaction of an audience upon the speaker; it arises from human interest on his part. Audiences, like violins, catch and echo the tones that are on their own pitch. A character does not have to be interesting, to interest a sympathetic man. He is interested in everybody. This trait is native to him. It is instinctive, irresistible, compelling. The very presence of a fellow man stirs him. There is no other so sure a source of popularity. Our feelings are an investment that pays dividends in kind. Love and hate are only echoes. The extraordinary spell cast over men by Jesus of Nazareth is worthy of study by the public speaker. His winsomeness drew men to Him like a magnet. We read of how they "hung on his lips"; of how, "as he was drawing near the whole multitude began to rejoice"; He "could not be hid," for "the multitude thronged him"; they "followed him from all the cities." His enemies: "See how we prevail nothing; the world is gone after him." He ate and drank with publicans and sinners. He drew all classes equally, the rich and the poor, Joseph of Arimathea and Mary of Magdala. Mastery of men comes only to those that serve men.

> "Where can I find the Earl of Shaftesbury?"
> "Look for a tall man, helping somebody."
> He found him.

Can every public speaker acquire platform magnetism? Yes, within limits. There is, to be sure, a magic elusive quality born in some folk, that escapes analysis. Like protoplasm, the formula of ingredients may be known, but cannot be successfully compounded. Some incarnate devils have possessed platform magnetism to an eerie degree. Witness Elder L———, who drew throngs in religious revival meetings in New Haven in winter, and in summer is said to have run an opium joint in Philadelphia. Serpents charm, to bite.

There are degrees of platform magnetism. There is such a thing as "magnetic creeping." If a piece of iron be laid in the line of the earth's magnetic axis, it will eventually become magnetized. If struck a sudden blow, it will become magnetized at once. This is true of speakers. Devote your attention to the four elements I have named—health, humor, enthusiasm, sympathy—and strike for them with an iron will, and much may be won for you. In harmony with the phrases of physics, *magnetic lag, magnetic leak, magnetic saturation,* indolence and heartlessness will rob you of all you have gained not only in this, but in all other principles laid down in this book. No substitute has yet been found for hard work. The power to draw mankind to high ideals by the fascination of a winning personality is worth all it costs. Day and night, through cold and heat, in weariness and pain, in private study and in social contact, give yourself to these four sources of power. Mature years of application and the bleak rigors of self-sacrifice will reap their enduring reward. Quintilian:

> "Let us with all the affections of our heart endeavor to attain the very majesty of eloquence, than which the immortal gods have not imparted anything better to mankind, and without which all would be mute in nature, and destitute of the splendor of a perfect glory and future remembrance."

12

DICTION

Gray's *Anatomy* is authority for the statement that ordinarily more than four hundred separate movements of the tongue are used in one moment of speech. Therefore it should be under directing impulse and wise control. What an instrument the tongue is! First to display its activity at birth, and last to die; it never tires, and never grows old. James devotes one-fifth of his limited space to the tongue:

> "In many things we all stumble. If any stumbleth not in word, the same is a perfect man, able to bridle the whole body also. Now if we put the horses' bridles into their mouths that they may obey us, we turn about their whole body also. Behold, the ships also, though they are so great and are driven by rough winds, are yet turned about by a very small rudder, whither the impulse of the steersman willeth. So the tongue also is a little member, and boasteth great things. Behold, how much wood is kindled by how small a fire! And the tongue is a fire: the world of iniquity among our members is the tongue, which defileth the whole body, and setteth on fire the wheel of nature, and is set on fire by hell. For every kind of beasts and birds, of creeping things and things in the sea, is tamed, and hath been tamed by mankind: but the tongue can no man tame; it is a restless evil, it is full of deadly poison."

Your wisdom determines what you shall say; your tongue, how you shall say it. Any idea can be expressed, so rich is our language in nice shades of meaning, if one will take time to think how to express it. Fine shades of meaning in the speaker's thought and sentiment are matched by fine distinctions between words. So ingeniously may one's vocabulary be manipulated, that it can serve not only as a sword, but as a shield, and the cynic's definition of language is, that it is "a device for concealing thought." Therefore speak right for the sake of the end you have in view. Thick or slipshod enunciation defeats your purpose. Nature has furnished the tools for the entire speech structure, from framework to finished moulding. Tongue, teeth, palate, trachea, jaw, lungs, roof of mouth—all contribute.

You must speak accurately, for the sake of your influence. Our speech is derived from environment. From our earliest words, we speak what we do hear. It is for this reason that you owe it to your hearers to afford them a chaste and worthy example of style. There is a saying of Jeremiah's in the book of *Lamentations* that has been misunderstood: "Mine eye affecteth my soul." The careless reader would reverse it, to read: "My soul affecteth mine eye," illustrating the influence of one's feelings over one's facial expression. But that is not the prophet's meaning: he teaches that we are what we see. Every master of correct speech is a literary benefactor to the community, furnishing an example to all that are ambitious to succeed. Poor speakers are made by poor models.

Learn to speak accurately for the sake, also, of your future. Good English soon becomes habitual. "How use doth breed a habit in a man!" We judge the general culture of a man by the English he uses. Your standards of expression today are fixing your permanent style. Your vocabulary, your apt turns of speech will grow by acquisition and use. A good golfer needs more clubs than a beginner, for whom a mid-iron and putter are enough. A cabinet maker uses tools that an apprentice doesn't even know the names of. Words are like money: the more you have, the more you can do with them. Victor Hugo had an enormous vocabulary. The average man has not over one or two thousand words in his vocabulary. Trench said that the English workingman used not more than three hundred. Yet some dictionaries contain in all about a half million. Milton, we are told, used eight thousand; Shakespeare, fifteen thousand.

Therefore, among the effective elements of style in public discourse, I name words first. Wrote Wilson: "The knowledge of words is the gate of scholarship." The words in our English Bible are the premier treasures of our language. Next to Shakespeare's revelation of human nature, his glory lies in his words. One-syllable words, quite familiar to us, he uses in new relations, as:

"The heart I sway by, and the mind I bear,
Shall never sag with doubt, nor shake with fear."

We can say: "If we speak the truth, we need not fear the future."
Shakespeare: "Truth hath a quiet breast." He has the faculty
of saying much in few words:

"Hear more than thou showest,
Speak less than thou knowest,
Lend less than thou owest."

In borrowing words from the mighty quivers of Shakespeare,
Milton, or Spenser, though the language has not materially
changed since 1600, it will be safe to consult the dictionary where
doubt exists whether they be obsolete.

Words must be chosen that are appropriate to the purpose in
view, words characterized by "purity, propriety, and precision."
Make your motto the injunction painted on the city curb: "Keep
Clear." It is not enough to speak correctly, nor even succinctly.
The old lady, asking when the next trains were to leave, was
confused by the agent's reply: "Two to two; and two: two."
She wondered whether he was the whistle, she said. Inexpensive
handbooks of diction and word usage are available in bookstores
as well as on the paperbound racks at drug stores. The speaker
does well to spend spare moments with them. Here can only be
given some samples of precise diction with which the speaker
should make himself thoroughly familiar, as a beginning. A few
words such as the following, expressing nice distinctions of meaning, should be made familiar. A *vocation* is one's calling; *avocation,* one's hobby. We speak of a *luxurious* home, but of *luxuri-
ant* vegetation. A thing that is *likely* to happen may be agreeable
or not agreeable; a thing that is *liable* to occur, is something to be
dreaded. There are some words for which, if one is not familiar
with them, he must use a whole phrase to express his meaning:
viscous, meaning half way between solid and liquid; *translucent,*
meaning an object through which the light passes, but which is
not *transparent,* so as to be seen through; *continuous,* i.e., contin-
uing without interruption, vs. *continual,* i.e., intermittent. In
science the word *abiogenesis* signifies life that has not come from
preceding life. In theology, the *Immaculate Conception* does
not mean, as it is so often incorrectly used by newspapers and

disputative theologians, that Jesus was born of a virgin; it means
that Mary His mother was as sinless as He was. *The Dictionary
of Phrase and Fable* will be found an invaluable help. So will
Roget's *Thesaurus* in any one of its many editions and Crabb's
English Synonyms. Word finders and guides to words often mis-
pronounced are numerous, and the finished orator has one or
two of them on his desk and often in his hand. A vocabulary will
either develop or atrophy; it will not stand still.

Clearness is necessary, also, because some words have more than
one meaning. The word *sleeper* has three. Some words are so
clear in themselves that their very use illuminates the whole subject. Shakespeare:

> "List his discourse of war, and you shall hear
> A fearful battle rendered you in music."

Suit your language to your audience. Familiarity with section-
alism gives the traveler an advantage in this respect. In the East,
there is a tin *pail,* a coal *hod,* and a well-*bucket:* out West, all
three are *buckets.* A *bag* in the East is a *sack* in the West. Down
East in the country, the word *convey* may become *fetch* or *lug;*
out West it is *pack;* down South it is *tote; carry* is safe everywhere. When they speak of a *walnut* in southern New England,
they mean what elsewhere is called a *hickory-nut.*

Use dignified words. Journalese should be used but sparingly,
if at all. Slang vulgarizes speech. But if you use it, see that it is
up to date. Seek diligently just the right word, until its use becomes a habit, as a stone-mason looks for the stone to fill each
niche. Make careful study of synonyms and antonyms, for whose
use special dictionaries exist. Dr. Kerr B. Tupper says, "A man's
culture is tested by his adjectives." This suggestion will be found
helpful: get a small blank book, and enter in two columns, in
the left good, and in the right disparaging, adjectives that are
not yet in your every-day vocabulary. When you write or speak,
incorporate them.

Adopt words of strength. Elegance, smoothness, are important;
but only as adjuncts to strength. How often, as the spinner of
talk reflects on his public utterance, he finds that "sad memory
weaves nothing but leaves." Virile words brace the hearer like
a tonic. Short sentences make for vitality. A simple direct style,

couched in virile Anglo-Saxon words, is demanded by hearers today. Mid-Victorian latinisms, labored epigrams, even "poetic imagery," are of a past day. Remember that word-power is often carried by verbs. Study with some care the use of verbs in vigorous poetry; James Weldon Johnson's poem "The Creation" is an excellent example. Take one of your own written addresses and study the verbs; try to replace some of them with ones which are more colorful, more precise, more vivid. Strike straight from the shoulder, aiming for the spot between the two eyes. We no longer define a man as Spencer did:

> "Man is a transcendental ideation of solidaric interceptive autochthonal redaction and orgasmic individualism of mobilized aggressus and noctic and dianoctic plasticities of intellectivity; i.e., man is an ectypical macrocosmic modality of ultraneous and fusiform differentiation, spontaneously racemated into homogenous individuality."

Leave to scientific discussion the technical phraseology of science. Egotism may parade on the platform great swelling words, but men of intelligence do not need them.

> An old negro, says the Chicago *Times-Herald*, was driving a drummer to the station in a southern city, when this conversation took place.
> "Boss, if you kin say over a few big words on de way down, I'd be extremely disobliged to you."
> "How big words do you want?"
> "Cain't get 'em too big, boss. I's a powerful hand to remember big words, and git 'em off when a calamitous occasion predominates."
> "Do you expect to find use for them this morning?"
> "'Reckon I does, sah. My son Abraham works down to de depot, and whenever I comes forward he tries to show off ober me, and make me feel small. He'll try it on dis mawnin', an' I jest want to be fixed to paralyse his desirability."
> We had about a half mile to go, and before we reached the depot I gave him a large and choice assortment of Webster's longest vocabularic curiosities.
> When we drew up at the platform, Abraham was there and also a dozen white people who were to go out on the train. It was a good opportunity for the son to show off, and he realized it, and came forward and waved his arm and shouted: "Yo' dar, ole man; hain't I told you about four hundred times not to sagacitate dat stupendous ole vehicle in de way ob de omnibus? Some ole niggers don't seem to hab no mo' idea ob de consanguinity ob rectitude dan a squash."
> "Was yo' spoken to me, sah?" quickly demanded the father, as he stood up and glared at Abraham.
> "Ob cose I was."

"Den sah, I wish you to distinctly understand dat when de cooperation ob de imperialism seems to assimilate a disreputable infringement
of hereditary avariciousness, I shall retract my individuality, but not
befo', not befo', sah."

Abraham's eyes hung out, his complexion became ash-color, and his
knees bent under him as if the springs were about to give way. It was
a moment before he could utter a sound, and then he reached for my
trunk with the muttered observation: "Things am gettin' so mixed
up I can't tell whedder I am de son or his father."

Use familiar words. Words, like clothes, are for the purpose
of attracting attention not to themselves but to the thought that
they adorn. Dr. Johnson's polysyllabic latinisms would bring
ridicule from a modern audience. A speaker that used them
would be believed to be "showing off." Note that Lincoln's
"Gettysburg Address" is like the parables of Jesus in that neither
needed long, complex polysyllables to convey sublime truths.
Great language may be simple language; profound teaching may
be phrased in the speech all men commonly employ.

Learn to use picture words, and to use them naturally. Cultivate imagination. A figure of speech, like a longer illustration,
must not seem to have been "lugged in." No other words so
color literature, or clarify ideas. Written language began with
hieroglyphics. Such words are the familiar speech of the savage,
as of the poet, both of whom live near the heart of nature. Study
the Indian Tagore, and the poet of the plains, Vachel Lindsay.
When we say that a writer has beauty of style, we mean that he
employs figurative language. Convey an incident, a character
sketch, a history, a travel experience, by a picture word. Reading poetry will enlarge the vocabulary, and open the eyes of the
mind. There are two sorts of picture words, the metaphor and
the simile. The simile is a comparison, being introduced by *like*
or *as*. Mark Twain quoted a friend in a simile: "Turner's paintings are like a tortoise-shell cat having a fit in a platter of toma-
toes." A metaphor substitutes the picture for the word, without
the intervening comparison. A French writer: "The sky is a
letter, of which the sun is the seal; when night comes on and re-
moves the seal, we read in a thousand starry letters that God is
love." Allegory and parable are extended metaphors and similes.
Do not drag your figure so far that it becomes frayed around
the edges. Do not mix figures, either with unfigurative language,

or with each other. Avoid Irish "bulls" and cheap puns. If you pun, use only such play on words as is really diverting or forcible. The Bible and Shakespeare abound in brilliant puns.

Select your words carefully. Enlarge your vocabulary. A young minister recalls his first speech in prayer-meeting: "If we're going to do something, we ought to do something that's worth something." That speech had more sagacity than vocabulary. When you hear a yeasty new word, or read it, look it up, if not sure of its meaning, and bring it into service at the first opportunity. Use a new word three times, and you will use it spontaneously. To your list of adjectives, you are ready now to add a list of nouns, selected for their variety, appositeness and novelty; novelty to yourself, but not so bizarre as not to be understood by intelligent readers. Translate other languages, and you will be led to take down from your mental shelves many words hitherto unused. Long after Cicero was recognized as the leading orator of the Roman Empire, he continued carefully to find some minutes in his intensely busy day for the art of translating poetry and prose from Greek into Latin. This he did solely for the strength it gave to his vocabulary. If you know two languages, even slightly, translate. Rufus Choate read carefully every day a page of the dictionary. A young Englishman from the mines, a member of my congregation, who had had no advantages of family or early culture, carried a dictionary in his pocket, and studied it at every spare moment. No better use could be made of otherwise wasted moments. By the time he finished preparatory school, he was one of the best preachers in the state; by the time he reached college, he won all the debating prizes. A less than average student, public speaking was the passion of his life, on which he labored night and day.

Look well to your enunciation and pronunciation. Fowler in *The Art of Speech Making:* "Probably half the people who inhabit the earth have some impediment in their speech." As careless writing makes a letter illegible, so muggy speaking makes a speech unintelligible. Both are owing to ill-formed words, and their maker deserves the general contempt that is felt for his work. A United States Adjutant General, during the war: "A great number of men have failed at camp because of their inability to articulate clearly. A man who cannot impart his ideas to his command in clear distinct language, and with sufficient volume of voice to be heard reasonably far, is not qualified to give command upon which human life will depend." Of what value is it that you know what you mean, when no one else can?

Enunciation is distinctness of utterance, giving not only the vowels, but also the consonants, their par value. To clip a syllable may be as great a crime as to clip a guinea. Have you ever played the game of *Scandal?* It is a revelation of the average jumbled enunciation. The first person in the row whispers a sentence, and the rest, each to his neighbor, repeat what they have heard. "This is a worm: do not step on it" became "This is a warm doughnut; step on it." A boy, when asked to illustrate the words "kith and kin": "A man asked my sister, 'May I kith you?' and she said, 'You kin.'" The commonest errors are: clipping words; running them together, a practice that makes the French language so difficult for the foreigner to understand; changing vowel sounds, as Europeans do with English words; and not opening the mouth. If an engineer were as reckless with his pipes and valves as most speakers are with the use of their throat and lips, there would be an explosion. It is the accepted opinion that vowel sounds are the chief sufferers in faulty enunciation. But I think the consonantal sounds are as frequently smothered. It is true that our language is vexatiously puzzling. Imagine a foreigner trying to pronounce accurately the lines:

> "Though the tough cough and hiccough plough me through,
> Through life's dark lough my course I'll still pursue."

Pronounce all of the above words as any one of them is pronounced, and note the result.

Pronunciation is speaking the word according to the best usage, as determined by the dictionary. The habit of skimming books for their story, with no attention to the style, is partly responsible for mispronunciation in speech. Form the habit of hearing, in the mind, the word as it should be pronounced, without moving the lips, or uttering a sound, letting "the ear *feel* the sound." Pronounce the whole word. It is as faulty to say *priess* or *munss* for priests or months, as to say "goin' an' comin'." Practice on the familiar tongue-twisters, "Theophilus Thistle," "She sells sea-shells," "Seven croquey-roqueys down a steep slope sliding," "He thrusts his fists against the posts, and still insists he sees the ghosts." Be fair to the vowels. In a New England college town, it is well to adopt the Italian *ä*, as in Great Britain; but in the West, the speaker may not wish to go farther than the dictionary, which limits it to comparatively few words, as *laugh, half, plant, staff, demand, aunt, wrath,* etc. It would sound stilted, out West, to use the Italian ä in the sentence:

"I can't laugh half enough at that calf on its path to the bath,"

even though bidden by the dictionary to do so—to pronounce the words so. Watch for the long *e's:* find out what your dictionary says about the words, *medieval, fetish, economical, evangelical.* And the double *o: roof, root, hoof, woof, soon.* No other letter has received such neglect as *u,* which is to be pronounced like ew and eu in *few* and *beauty,* in such words as *tune, duke, suit, nude, Tuesday, institution, duty.* As we already say *cue,* we must also say *due,* as we say *few,* let us also say *new.* Diphthongs must be pronounced, both letters receiving their due, in *diphtheria, diphthong, naphtha.* The last word, however, is now often written without the first h.

"Words are instruments of music: an ignorant man uses them for jargon; but when a master touches them, they have unexpected life and soul. Some words sound out like drums; some breathe memories sweet as flutes; some call like a clarionet; some shout a charge like trumpets; some are sweet as children's talk; others rich as a mother's answering back."

Abbe Ernest Dimnet tells with amusement in his *Art of Thinking* of the man who offered ten thousand dollars could he but read Greek. Alas, notes the Abbe, only the man himself could by his own efforts acquire that skill. So it is with words. They are the tools of the orator's profession, but only he can provide himself with them and only he can keep them bright and sharp and ever renewed. Anyone who has heard a man speak—any man, schooled or unschooled—who brings to his speaking the background of having read in the dictionary a few minutes a day does not have to be persuaded that this habit is worth while. It shows in every sentence. So does its opposite.

13

SUBJECTS AND TREATMENT

You can build a given theme, or, if you are a preacher, a chosen text, as an architect builds stones, into any kind of a structure. You can build a palace, a garage, a cathedral, or a henhouse. The purpose in view will determine the choice of a subject. And the subject will determine, to a degree, the treatment it is to get. When Michelangelo received the order of Julius II for the design which was to hold the papal mausoleum, the great sculptor spent nine months in the quarries selecting his marbles. Success loves care. Levity in the topic forbids greatness in the treatment. A speech is, like a great tree,

> "produced too slowly ever to decay,
> Of form and substance too magnificent to be destroyed.
> 'Twould seem that, perched upon its topmost bough,
> With outstretched fingers man might reach the stars."

The end will determine the means.

Select your subject with great care. It determines in large measure the force and clearness of the flow of the whole discourse. The speaker must know exactly what he means by his topic, and it must be so worded that everybody else shall.

Let the title be brief, whether it is advertised or not. A brief topic will be more easily remembered by both speaker and hearers; will serve clearness; and it will have its influence on the speaker himself in making for definiteness, force, conciseness. It should be so framed as to arouse interest and kindle curiosity. It cannot be too often emphasized that an audience like to think for themselves, as every experienced speaker knows. Predigested mental fodder softens the mind, in place of nourishing it. It is better to kindle opposition than indifference.

"Hunger is the best sauce." Every one has something of the explorer in his make-up. The Holy Grail must be worth the quest of the crusader.

The topic must contain the theme, without revealing its substance. It must be true to the subject-matter, and not promise what it cannot perform, like a misplaced guidepost. Speeches of ambitious beginners are sometimes like the advertisement of Barnum's circus: you know you will get something, but you feel pretty sure that it will not be so good as it is advertised to be. While the title must be true to the subject-matter, it must not be so transparent as to uncover its treasures. One man's topic will make an old truth new; another's will make a new truth old. Examples of good topics are Chalmers' *The Expulsive Power of a New Affection;* Spurgeon's *Little Dogs;* Talmage's series on *The Wedding Ring;* Munger's *Music as a Revelation;* Wunder's *Light Housekeeping, or Lighthouse Keeping?* A student of mine, who was to speak on civic morals, announced: *A Tale of Three Cities.*

It is well for the minister to map out a three or five years' course of topics. He can thus lay out a systematic body of instruction, which shall be both comprehensive and progressive, and carry it through. The teaching function is your most valuable gift. A congregation will thrive and grow under such a leader. We all want to learn. Sheep that are fed do not leap the fence. A grain bin is the most secure corral. Teaching-ministers are honored by their congregations, and cherished by posterity. The sermons of Robertson of Brighton, Alexander Maclaren of Manchester, are still eagerly read, as those of Jefferson of New York and Truett of Dallas will continue to be. So let the wise minister plan a whole course of sermons, to be developed progressively through a series of years. He will of course provide room for special appeals; but he will not suffer these to be so many that they will swamp his program. For the seasonal psychology, as we think more naturally along certain directions at each season, it is well for him to divide the year into periods, somewhat perhaps after the following fashion: after vacation, in September and October, stress local church plans and activities, in the spirit of loyalty to the church as a divine institution. In November and December, as the Christmas season approaches, he will lead the thought of his people farther afield, and inspire them with the world outlook, through missions. He may begin the new year with teaching the significance of the great Christian doctrines, as they are held by the churches, but not clearly apprehended by most church members. In February, March and April, he will stress evangelism, leading up to the incoming of new members on Easter Sunday. To set before his church, and specially before the new members, the real aims of the Christian life, he may devote the summer months, before the summer vacation, to the multifarious and growing demands of social service, for which the summer season both in the city and in vacation resorts offers excellent opportunities. If the projected course be for five years, each specific subject can be progressively treated under five topics, like chapters in a book. In this way, the theme can be adequately treated; repetition avoided; various aspects emphasized. The preacher will be spared the vexed question: "What shall I preach about, next?" The hit-or-miss method hits some things too often; and misses some things that should be hit.

Welcome suggestions as to your theme, but allow no one to dictate to you what you shall speak about. Your independence is vital. When the prophet Balaam refused to curse the armies of Israel, he gave King Balak the threefold policy on which his public deliverances were based; he would speak what Jehovah told him, only what Jehovah told him, and all that Jehovah told him. (Num. 23:12; 23:26; 24:13.) His program was identical with that of our law courts: to "speak the truth, the whole truth, and nothing but the truth." The preacher must be too sane for superstition, and too sincere for sanctimoniousness. A "call" to the ministry means that education, observation, timeliness, and the spirit of service join to lead him to choose that profession. When these things combine to lead any man to choose a profession or a business career, they are God's call to him.

Whence shall a public speaker get his themes? From the special needs of his audience, and the demands of the occasion, which must always be first with him. His selection of a theme will be limited by his personal experience. He will be a constant reader of the daily newspaper to keep himself informed of those current topics on which the public mind is dwelling, and of the magazines, and best sellers in fiction. The philosophy of life, as it bears on the people of his day, is to be found in the popular novels. Many an interesting topic will suggest itself to him on his business and professional calls, and in conversation. "As iron sharpeneth iron, so a man sharpeneth the countenance of his friend." If Moses, or Emerson, or Montaigne should read tonight's paper, he would exclaim: "I told you so!" No commentary on philosophy or on the Bible can displace the daily paper. It is life's mirror. Lay down this book for a moment; and pick up the latest paper; on the front page you will find three subjects: love, fear, and finance. Love is the source of all that is printed about religion and marriage, with the weal and woe that hover about them. Fear is the basis of international relationships and courts of justice. Money dictates all that is written about business, commerce, and municipal advance. Love, fear and money are so interlocked that each affects the activities of the other two. Now, if these three passions or instincts are foremost in the news of the daily press reports, they indicate the trend of public thought, and what the speaker must discuss if he is to find his audience and influence them. The speaker's range of themes is as wide as human life. That is the reason public sentiment lies in his keeping. It is why the gospel has been committed to the hands of men, not to angels' hands.

Repeat often, of course to a different audience, those speeches that are a success. It is almost impossible to tell beforehand whether a speech is going to be a success or not, and it is frequently inexplicable even to the most experienced speaker why an audience receive an address with the favor or the disfavor which they manifest toward it. But they are the only competent judges, and he will be wise to leave the decision, for or against repetition, to them; and to follow their lead. The idea that a speech is a speech, and that one carefully prepared talk will "go" as well as another, is far from the facts, and will bring to him that cherishes it a rude awakening. An English farmer told me that in his native town the parish incumbent kept his sermons in a "gunny-sack," and on Sunday morning he would give the bag a swift kick, and the first sermon that leaped out he would preach. "Sometimes," remarked my friend, "he would

preach the same sermon two Sundays in succession, but the congregation didn't know the difference." Doubtless. Laziness is
its own reward. The advantage of repeating a taking address
is that it improves with age, like wine that is ripened in the
wood. Theodore Parker said to a reporter: "I never repeat an
old sermon; I repeat only those that are always new." In that
case, the oldest is the newest, like the moonrise, or the spring.
John Jasper, the eloquent Negro preacher, made his fame by
the sermon, *De sun do move,* which he repeated more than two
hundred times. Conwell's *Acres of Diamonds* was its own best
advertisement, and brought to Temple College millions of dollars. I heard D. L. Moody's sermon on *The Holy Spirit* five
times, with unflagging interest. In view of what has been said,
it is well for a speaker to have one or two labeled envelopes,
in which he places the notes of his most effective addresses, according to their grouping, so that they shall be ready at hand.

Probe to the heart. The surgeon that is afraid to excise to the
root a malignant growth is a less odious coward than the speaker
that deals half heartedly with a hearer's faults. Let the over-
gentle apologetic orator know that an audience respects the man
that deals honestly and uncompromisingly with them, and de-
spises the man that is afraid of them. Court favor and you lose
it. Don't be like the preacher of whom Spurgeon told his students, who warned his hearers that if they did not repent they
would "go to a place that politeness forbids me to mention."
On the other hand, scolding defeats its own end. Audiences are
not won to new opinions by badgering them. Sympathy and
hardness are inconsistent with each other. In ancient Wales, the
scold was compelled to wear a mask—as you muzzle dogs. A
speaker that is cross with his audience loses all authority with
them.

Choose large themes. It is easier swimming in deep water. If
you are a minister, preach about your Master. In the Puritan
phrase, let there be *aliquid Christi* in every sermon. Spurgeon,
whom someone called "the Prime Minister of England": "The
true grandeur of preaching is to have Christ grandly exalted in
it."

The treatment of the theme. Above and beyond all rules
that I shall lay down for evolving the theme, after it has been

chosen as above, is an injunction that is so simple that it can be couched in a single word; and yet so important that it deserves a volume. That rule is: THINK. Counsel is perished from the prudent. A gift of fluency, pressure of other duties, a too eager enthusiasm to rush into the body of the discourse, or just old-fashioned laziness, make nine-tenths of our speaking in public mediocre, through an unwillingness to sit down at the very beginning and concentrate the whole mind, to the oblivion of all else, on the chosen subject and its development. If Dr. Cadman of New York, himself one of the two best known ministers in America, were asked why he pronounced Dr. George A. Gordon of Boston America's greatest preacher, I suppose he would answer that it is the thought which he has devoted to his sermons that has given him primacy.

There should be a variety of treatment as well as a variety of themes. Resist determinedly your inclination to confine yourself to that which is easiest for you. Otherwise, you will fall into a personal groove that will rob you of the charm of your freshness. To illustrate: there are five differing methods of developing a sermon theme. The text, the topic, the purpose in mind, or the occasion, will determine which of the five is the best, under the circumstances. The first three methods depend upon the Bible selection that is chosen. These are known as the textual, the expository, and the inferential, methods. Textual preaching discusses, usually in their order, each clause, or, in a short text, each word, of the verse. This was Spurgeon's method. Suppose one choose the question from Ezekiel: "Why will ye die?" Each word makes a separate division: (1) Reasons for spiritual suicide; (2) The obstinacy of a wrong determination; (3) Individual responsibility for failure in life; (4) The penalty of sin. The expository method is like the textual method, except that it is extended to a longer passage: a paragraph or chapter instead of a verse. Expository preaching is the method of Dr. G. Campbell Morgan of Los Angeles. An excellent example of it is Drummond's *Love the Greatest Thing in the World*. The inferential method resembles the expository method, except that it follows the passage more loosely. The fourth method, the doctrinal, does not necessarily require a text. Dr. Fosdick's famous sermon on *Fundamentalism* is an illustration of this style. The fifth is the topical method, in which the topic takes precedence; the text, if any, being used as a motto. A text often receives torturous treatment at the hands of the popular topical preacher. He might choose as his theme: *Life as a Game of Golf,* and take as his text: "He will turn and toss thee like a ball into a large country." The best topical preaching never does violence to the original meaning of the text: it uses it only as a suggestion. Topical preaching is best adapted to the Sunday night popular service of a down-town congregation.

Every speech contains four parts, arranged in the following order. First, there is the announcement of the theme which, in the case of a sermon that is introduced by a text, may follow the introduction. In all formal addresses, the theme should always be clearly announced, either by the speaker or by the introducing chairman. People naturally want to know what a man is going to talk about, and not have to guess for themselves after they have been traveling the road with him for fifteen minutes or more. After the introduction in a speech has been finished, it is often well to repeat the announcement of the theme, for the sake of clearness and for the benefit of late-comers.

Vary your introduction, as well as your topic and treatment. Variety is sometimes served by omitting the introduction altogether, and starting the race from the tape. One of the happiest introductions is a reference to the local situation, specially in an after dinner talk, where a witty "slam" on the toastmaster, or preceding speaker, is appreciated. The environment, or some recent incident that is fresh in the minds of the audience, may make an appropriate stepping-stone from which to climb into the body of your address. Sometimes it may be necessary, in the introduction, to explain your choice of a topic or text, or to clear up difficulties that are in the public mind about the theme. Cicero said an introduction should render the audience friendly, attentive, and teachable. Think on each of these qualifications: *friendly, attentive,* and *teachable.* Then study one of your introductions, or plan your next one, with an eye to *creating each* of these attitudes. Decide which sentences will accomplish each task. Everything is appropriate in an introduction that prepares the way for, or leads up to, your subject, with the proviso that it must always be brief, and not made up of a personal apology. But do not hesitate beginning with an apology when one is due: if you are late, if you are for some reason unprepared for what you meet, if you suffer temporary physical handicap. Only be sure that your apology is straitforward, honest, and not meant to gain sympathy.

The main body of the speech, lying between the introduction and the conclusion, is an opening up of the theme, with an analysis for its framework, and containing illustration and application. To the great majority of speakers, an analysis, prepared after the selection of the theme, and before the introduction and conclusion, is essential. While there are a few minds so constituted that they can prepare and deliver an effective address without the bone-frame, yet most speakers will wander about and arrive nowhere without one. It should generally contain from two to five main divisions, with two or three subheads under each marked respectively, I, i, (i) etc. If you carry a brief to the desk, it will help to catch your eye more quickly if the main divisions are underscored as to their captions in colored pencil. A flexible rule with some speakers is to average one quotation and one illustration in each main division.

The conclusion, which, like the introduction, is an integral part of your speech, should be carefully prepared, not only in the interest of an effective final impression, but also to make sure of stopping at the crucial moment without dribbling. It may be composed in one of three different ways, or of all three combined. You may drive home the teaching contained in the main body of your address, applying to your hearers the principles that have been stated. Or, it may contain a telling illustration, or quotation, that shall both illuminate the subject and stir the feelings. Or, it may be a résumé of your thought, summing up the argument point by point, in a few sentences. In order to cultivate skill in analysis, it will be well for the student to copy out the theme, introductory thought, and division-heads of the addresses of some speaker famous for his clear-cut analyses. Charles H. Spurgeon is an excellent model in this respect.

Distinguish for public speech between an essay and an oration. Essays are intended to be read, orations to be spoken. But essays may also be delivered in public, as at some scientific gatherings; or before women's clubs, whenever the occasion calls for special care in style or close reasoning. An essay, however, lacks the force, condensation, and drive of an oration. The former affords instruction to the mind, the latter moves upon the will and the emotions. The most important thing in any public utterance is that it shall convey the idea. The two most important ways to convey the idea are by being interesting, and being in earnest.

14

ILLUSTRATION

I closed the last lecture by saying that the best ways to convey an idea are by making it interesting, and by being in earnest. Let us now go a step farther, and add that one of the most effective ways of being interesting is by the use of illustration. We have not progressed far from the childhood of the race in that respect. The earliest languages of which we have record—the Japanese and Chinese, and the cuneiform hieroglyphics—were picture languages. Each character is a symbol. The second letter of the Hebrew alphabet, for example, beth, ב, is the word for *house,* and its shape is that of a roof. The Japanese character for *West,* 西, represents the sun going down behind a tree. The ancient troglodyte intended literally to make you see what he meant. As poetry is older than prose, and the dance older than the procession, so illustration is the oldest form of narrative. The modern child can draw better than he can write. The deaf naturally speak with their fingers. The realtor's map, the salesman's pencil, which he takes out whether he has anything to draw or not, are evidence that one must see a thing first in order to want it. Euclid employed the geometrical diagram to teach the abstractions of mathematics. AEsop and La Fontaine by their fables introduced childhood to the fearsome and fascinating doings of the animal kingdom, and thus anticipated Darwin, *Uncle Remus, Alice in Wonderland, The Jungle Books,* and Ernest Thompson-Seton. The genius in the childhood days of the race who grouped the stars into constellations unsealed a picture book of unfailing delight, and taught astronomy by illustration. Defoe wrote *Robinson Crusoe* only as an introduction to the long religious tract which originally completed the story; but the world loved the illustration more than they did the sermon; a fact that ought to serve as a warning to the preacher! The novel is only an illustration of ethical truth in the large.

Mankind's chief interest is in morals and religion. Much genius and learning of the world have been devoted to their service as friends or as foes. Every political and international question is basically a moral issue. What is every painting, from the days of the old masters to the modern academician, every statue that has been called from the quarry of a Phidias or a Rodin but an illustration of human life under the sway and tug of moral forces? Abstract thought is made clear by appropriate illustration. That is why books are made with illustrations in them. The "morgue" has now become a necessity to every newspaper office. We all like to look at pictures and do our own thinking about them. The moving picture trust controls American ideals. Illustration is remembered when argument is forgotten. Example overtops precept. Bible history is a literary picture gallery.

Illustrations capture an audience where logic fails to convince. Sophistry, well illustrated, will often prevail over sound argument unadorned: read the two speeches in the grey light of the next morning, and see what you think about them! Illustrations are particularly effective in debate when the whole audience is to render the decision. Hearing is interesting; seeing is believing. We have "recourse to reason"; but we dwell in our imagination. In the case of a lecture course or preaching, where the same audience is to be kept interested, it is well occasionally to attain variety by making the whole speech out of a single illustration. It is a pictorial edition. Bunyan's *Pilgrim's Progress,* the most popular book ever written, is one prolonged illustration of life under the guise of a journey. The pageant, and the Sunday night drama sermons, are expansions of the idea. An allegory is only a prolonged parable, and a fable a teaching-myth. The Bible stories of *Esther* or *Jonah* could be rendered by the minister, with their present-day implications, as a continued parabolic narrative, a chapter or connected incident for each week. A parable from *Judges* or *Luke* may be amplified with suggestive detail and synchronized to modern conditions. An audience listens with surprising attention to "sermons in stones, books

Illustration   111

in the running brooks," based on historical incidents, songs, books, concrete objects. Henry Ford's revival of the schoolhouse of *Mary's Lamb* calls to mind the story of how a great Boston church was saved by that lamb's wool.

Good illustrations are as varied in character as the truths they embellish. Their supply is inexhaustible. So varied are the occasions and the topics that confront the speaker, that it is the part of prudence to lay by him in store a nestful of such assorted nuts to crack. He is invariably asked to give "just a word of welcome" at the beginning of a program, or at public receptions to eminent citizens. The uninitiated fancy that such talks can be thrown off at any time, without preparation. As a matter of fact, they are among the hardest of his duties. To give novelty and variety to forty such talks is more difficult than to prepare forty half-hour addresses on varied themes. Many times must an attorney plead before the same court, on the same sort of case, or the clergyman preach a funeral sermon before the same persons. To say the same thing in a different way is an intellectual and spiritual feat requiring not only a versatile imagination, but a fund of material that would furnish an essayist for a lifetime. "Repetition waxes to vexing wind." The fact that such talks are brief makes them doubly difficult.

The problems of a lyceum lecturer are as great, but they are quite different from those of the professor or the clergyman. The making of introductions alone that shall meet the requirements of an habitual audience accustomed to the manner, voice and temperament of the speaker is most difficult. Make three or four thousand, and you will see! This variety and appositeness must be maintained throughout the divisions and subdivisions of the address, and culminate in an emotional and logical climax. To cap a thousand appeals to the uneducated or the unregenerate with new arguments or novel illustrations demands resources worthy of the mines of China. A preacher or a university professor, who is to interest auditors for a period of forty years—and these are long-lived callings—needs a collection of five or ten thousand illustrations and quotations from literature. "Well, there are the published volumes of anecdotes, and there are *Bartlett's Quotations*."

Most published volumes of anecdotes and quotations are valueless to a wide-awake speaker. For one thing, the fashion in such things changes from decade to decade. And most stories that appeal to a collector that has to sell them do not appeal to an audience that has to hear them. They lack variety, humor and human touch. They are not indexed in such a way as to cover the ground. To gather a thesaurus of telling illustrations is the work of a lifetime. Comparatively few of a lawyer's illustrations will be technically legal in themselves; or of a minister's, religious. A war bursts upon the world, famine or flood sweeps a nation, and the speaker must meet the new problems raised, and move in the new atmosphere created by them. To do this, he must have scores of appropriate illustrations at his hand. Strikes, pensions, divorce, child-labor, prison reform, courtship, thrift and expenditure, politics, family relations, modern amusement problems; and the demands of the Chautauqua platform, the after-dinner speech, the magazine contribution—all of these demand consideration from the platform, or from the ink-bottle. An experienced speaker can often tell at a glance what will strike or find an audience. Published books of quotations contain about the same proportion of wheat to stubble that one will find in a grain field. There are *Gems from Ruskin* that would have made Ruskin wonder whether he ever said them, and, if so, why. The collector's idea of a gem is not always that of the wearer.

The speaker or writer needs many more illustrations than he is likely to use soon. Not only are his subjects varied, but there are turns of thought, fine shades of meaning, specific applications, to be illustrated. You will do well, therefore, to provide yourself with a series of blank-page volumes, in which to enter them as you find them. You will have a separate Index volume, to record their titles under specific headings. Entered haphazard as they come, they will be numbered in order, each illustration having its own number above it, with its descriptive title. This title and number you can then enter under its main subject in the Index volume. Thus, if your theme is *Capital and Labor,* or *Matrimony,* or any other topic, you will turn to that theme-topic in your Index volume, glance over the titles, and look up the ones that seem specially appropriate to the subject you are considering. You will enter it by title and number in the notes of your address, and whenever you repeat that address, you can

Illustration 113

instantly refresh your memory in all the details of the illustration.

It is evident that such a collection is no less valuable to the magazine contributor or letter writer, who seeks to verify statistical or historical information without going through works of reference in a library. If you mark them in some way when you use them, you will avoid the danger of repeating them in another essay or speech to the same group. Professor Austin Phelps says that deadly repetition is more often criticized unfavorably by an audience than any other of the speaker's faults. Remember the church trustee that told Booker Washington, in justification for not paying their pastor's salary: "We paid for dem sermons last year." There are subjects recurring annually, like Christmas, Easter, the Fourth of July, New Year's Day, and the lodge or church financial canvass, that require fresh illustrative treatment. References to books in your library you will also index by title and page. The disadvantage of the customary envelope system is that you have to look through and read so many in the given pocket to find the one you are after.

Where shall appropriate illustrations be found? The man whose eyes are open will find them everywhere, the more extended the field the greater the variety. Beecher and Maclaren were like experienced prospectors. Their wealth was as varied as that of the Count of Monte Cristo. Ore from a thousand mines passes through the speaker's crucible, is smelted and becomes current coin. We read how some great preachers make their sermon analyses on Saturday night, or even on Sunday morning. But we must remember that the grist has been pouring into their mills every day and night of the year. Some illustrative sources are richer in their productiveness than others. You will learn how to find them. Your scent will be cultivated. Incidents from your own boyhood or personal experience have a peculiar charm, if told naturally and modestly. Next in interest are incidents from the lives of your friends and the mental adventures of your acquaintances. The thing that gives a biography charm, even if it be the biography of a comparatively obscure person, is the personal incidents connected with the lives and doings of well-known characters. Avoid unkind or embarrassing personalities, and trivialities. The daily paper will yield striking anecdotes. Yesterday a man in Oakland, California, whom I heard on the

radio, used effectively from that morning's papers the contrast-
ing views on God and immortality between Edison and Chauncey
Depew, giving vivid contemporary color by quoting two great
names on two great topics. History, biography, the latest scientific discoveries, afford admirable illustrations. Humorous anecdotes, bons mots, comments, have a useful place. We must remember that the taste of audiences changes in the matter of illustrations, as truly as in the style of their clothes. Public taste must
be satisfied, if an illustration is to accomplish anything. The
"classical" illustration is now largely out of vogue, and so are
pathetic stories. The former belonged to the old style "oratory,"
the latter is rejected for its sentimentality by the young as "sob
stuff." A bit of humor, a flash of satire, sparingly used, have universal appeal. Bible speakers use humor effectively. It is a false
notion that groans are more religious than laughter. Joy and
laughter ripple through the pages of the Bible like a mountain
brook. An early account of the personal appearance of our Lord
which says that He "was seen often to weep, but never to laugh"
is proved by that sentence to be spurious. Would sinners' dinner
parties, to which He was so often invited, have welcomed that
kind of a guest? Offensive traits may often be laughed out of a
man when threats only harden him. No one likes to appear ridiculous.

An anecdote must never be told for its own sake. Its application to the point in hand must be instantly evident. For that
reason, it should generally follow instead of precede the truth
it is to enforce. It is a skylight, not a foundation stone. It must
be tersely told, leaving as much as possible for the audience to
guess, giving only the relevant points. To trust the keen intelligence of an audience is to pay them a compliment, a compliment
which they generally deserve. To explain a story is felt by them
to be a veiled insult.

> "Strive not to say the whole! The poet in his art
> Must intimate the whole, and say the smallest part."

Interest and curiosity must be aroused by the first sentence. Keep
back the point till the end, and end the story the instant they
get the point. Add interesting sidelights, if they heighten the
force of your tale. Beware of incumbering it with impertinent

Illustration 115

details. Harry Lauder, in his description of how he and "Shack" (Colonel Shackleton) "nearly discovered the South Pole" has satirized the tedious story-telling bore, thus: "It was one Sunday mornin' when I was—I was very nearly goin' away to tell you a lie to begin with, for it wasna a Sunday at all! It was a Saturday forenoon, about half-past eleven—or a quarter to twelve—or maybe it was twelve o'clock—I don't know what time it was—I know it was the end of the week anyway—" etc. Your anecdote, too, must be interesting in itself; and new to a large part of the audience. In this day of political forensics and after-dinner yarns, it is hopeless to expect any story, unless you have made it up yourself, shall be new to all your audience. The safe rule is, never to tell a story that you have heard three times, or seen in *The Ladies Home Journal,* which everybody reads. People do not object to an occasional anecdote that they have enjoyed before, as they do not object to one or two of the old familiar songs at the close of a classical musical program. The story must have human touch, breathing the pathos and humor of the drama of life. Let it be as brief as possible. Incorporate illuminating quotations as sidelights on your story, just touching them in part as you pass.

Literary citations embellish the main body of an address. Epigrams and stanzas of poetry found in your general reading may be preserved for future use in a separate blank book kept for that purpose. No index will be required, as the quotation is to be written down under its appropriate heading. They must be pertinent, pungent, concise. Unless a quotation throbs with passion, sparkles with wit, or is a nugget of wisdom, there is no excuse for its use. The speaker can say it as well himself. Better a plain gold ring than to set it with a piece of glass. But a well-chosen quotation is a confirming testimony of a respectable witness, when a theory is on trial before an audience. If your reading is wise and wide, you will gradually lay by a galaxy of crown jewels that have come from the thrones of the world's highest culture. Classic literature is of course your best field. You can also gather quotations from leaders of present-day thought, whose names stand in the public mind, leaders whose very names are arguments. Your own thought gains prestige by the company it keeps. The reader may question your personal opinion; but how dispute Shakespeare, Moses, Luther?

Many addresses require no illustrations more extended than figures of speech. Others may need many. The occasion, the character of the audience, and the style of the oration will determine which, and how many, illustrations are to be used. Dress both yourself and your speech for the occasion. Don't fall into "anecdotage." Some speeches, such as historical, literary, biographical and allegorical addresses, are illustrations in themselves: no others are needed. Others, such as addresses to benevolent orders, business clubs, soldiers, firemen, baccalaureate addresses, funeral discourses, civic reform speeches, lend themselves to illustrations drawn from their nature or history, where a general anecdote would be weak.

Elucidation is an art, and demands patient study. It is often the conspicuously weak point in an otherwise good talk. Frequently one hears a speaker begin, "I can't tell a story." It is to help such that this chapter has been written. Determine at the outset that you will have nothing but the best. Choose one out of a thousand that lie about you, and even then you will have a limitless store from which to select. Only "rich pay dirt" is worth your mining and hauling away. A refined, exalted appeal may be degraded in the eyes of the audience, and the reputation of the speaker permanently cheapened, by an illustration of coarse vulgarity. We are known by the literary company we keep. Live among the great, associate with the noblest products of art and culture, and the sparks that fly from your anvil, as you hammer out your thought, will scintillate with light, and glow with fire.

Beecher said that illustrations acted like windows in the argument, letting in light. His sermons sparkle with them, and one anthology collected from his printed works contains more than two thousand.

The speaker must be warned, however, that illustrations are powerful instruments for woe as well as for weal. Poorly chosen ones may set the listener off on a mental journey far afield from that intended by the orator. The same illustration might suggest two or three implications, and the listener may not take the one which the speaker intended. Do not fall into the habit of picking illustrations out of the air at the moment they seem to

Illustration 117

be needed. Study those you use, and take only the ones which really illustrate and illuminate the point you wish to make. One speaker, wishing to illustrate the witness of creation to its Creator, chose to tell the story of Napoleon crossing the sea to Egypt. Listening one night to his officers discussing whether or not God existed, Napoleon suddenly thrust his arm heavenward toward the glittering stars, and exclaimed, "Gentlemen, if there be no God, who made these?" His point made, the speaker moved on. But how many of his listeners were lost in speculation as to what the officers replied?

15

UNITY, PROGRESS, BREVITY

A table with three legs keeps all three on the ground. If it had but two, it would tip over. If it had four, one of them might be in the air. The third has a necessary connection with the other two: it gives them an assured standing, justifies them. Without the other two, it would have no significance. The two supports that hold a like relation to public speech are Unity and Progress. Always think of them together. Neither of them by itself will bring success to an address, whether it be serious or informal.

The speech must be a unit. It is a great thing to aim at something, and hit it. The maharajah's polite servant said that the visiting British sahib "shot divinely, but Allah was merciful to the birds." One cannot expect an audience to be so charitable toward a speech that brings in no results. An address should present but one idea. Make each main division an integral part of the chosen theme, and each subdivision a legitimate sector of the main division, with nothing else to cloud the issue. Add all of these fractions together, and you have the subject entire. The heads of a discourse often group themselves about such unwritten questions as What? Why? How? and less often Who? Which? When? The square on this page represents the whole speech: the square in the middle is the theme; the vertical lines are the main divisions; the horizontal dotted lines are the subdivisions into which the main divisions are further divided, the dots representing thoughts, illustrations, quotations, etc., in these subdivisions. The square, i.e., the speech,

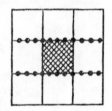

is a unit; all of the ideas must revolve around the central one, like the rings of Saturn: and illuminate it, like the moons of Jupiter. I have chosen the following blank outline from Shurter, in *Extempore Speech*, because it is the method I have myself followed, in practice, numbers and all, from the beginning:

```
    Topic ....................................................
Introduction
      1.
      2.
      3.
Discussion
    I .....................................................
      1.
      2.
      3.
      4.
    II ....................................................
      1.
      2.
      3.
      4.
    III ...................................................
      1.
      2.
      3.
      4.
Conclusion
      1.
      2.
      3.
```

Of course, only portions of this form need be used for individual speeches.

A speech is one side of a debate, and only one. To try to present both sides is to present neither. A modern philosopher tells us that the history of human thought demonstrates that the race averages one new idea for each generation. Under these circumstances it is well for the speaker to be modest, and if he come into possession of one strong, priceless thought, whether original or not is of no consequence, to abide by that thought for his half hour's talk, and develop it in its varied relations and applications. What it took a generation to produce ought to satisfy his intellectual cupidity for thirty minutes, as it is sure to satisfy his hearers. It is quality that he should be asking, not quantity; for as Beecher: "Some sermons seem to have been built by the mile." In great music, the theme is everything: one theme, in air and bass, major and minor, allegro and andante, crescendo and diminuendo, forte and pianissimo. One theme, and how many of them are notable? Schubert's *Serenade,* Gottschalk's *Last Hope,* Wagner's *Lohengrin,* Liszt's *Hungarian Rhapsodies,* Beethoven's *Moonlight Sonata,* each of these masterpieces of music is made famous by its theme. One theme. Our favorite Bible chapters have but one idea: I Corinthians 13, John 14, Psalm 119. Though the last named is the longest chapter in the Bible, with one hundred and seventy-six verses, all but three of them deal with one subject, the Law. The same is true of the world's great hymns: *Nearer, My God, to Thee, Just As I Am, America,* each stanza being a variation of the single thought of the hymn.

Your time is too short to present more than one idea. What can you do with a single hour, against the manifold thoughts of a week that call for the attention of the individuals of your audience? You, with your sublime ideal, are like Moses facing a nation worshiping a golden calf. Suppose he had tried to stand for the whole Ten Commandments that he held in his hand, instead of confining himself to the second one! Only an hour, or half hour, to produce an imperishable impression! Suppose an architect, or sculptor, or poet, were so closely limited in point of time. Yet the art of the speaker in public is greater than either of theirs. Concentration of the mind on a single idea is the key to achievement. Every one feels its driving force.

The idea must be a large one. A half hour is a long time in which to say nothing. Select the idea carefully. It is all you have. The reason the Church has concluded there must have been three wise men at the Nativity in Bethlehem, although the number of them is not mentioned in the gospel, is because the narrative says there were three gifts. Gold, frankincense and myrrh were such gifts as would call for an individual bearer each. One offering from one man is the world's standard, if the offering be valuable. Let the idea be greater than the speaker, one in which he can lose himself, so that he will be swept along by it, like a leaf in a gale; or like a derelict in an ocean current. A member of Spurgeon's congregation, taking a friend to hear the great London preacher for the first time: "What did you think of him?" The friend: "I thought nothing of him;" and then: "I thought nothing of Spurgeon; I thought only of Spurgeon's Saviour!"

Too many points weaken each point. "A multitude of sparks gives but a poor light." Some one has said that if you want to fasten a board to a wall, you do not throw a handful of nails at the board, but you hold one nail in place and hammer it home. The huge chrysanthemums of Japan are produced by culling out all of the small blossoms, to throw the strength into one perfect bloom. Every great campaign in history is waged about a single idea: "China for the Chinese!" "Cuba libre!" John Knox cried: "Give me Scotland, or else I die!" Back of the Emancipation Proclamation lay that scene years before, when Lincoln, a young man, saw slaves sold at the block: "If I ever get the chance, I'll hit that thing, and hit it hard!" Dualism may preserve, in philosophy, a safe balance of ideas, but it will wreck a speech. Even long comparisons, as between capital and labor, nationalism and internationalism, fundamentalism and modernism, distract and divide the thinking of an audience. Take one side, and save its converse for the next time. I preached a sermon at nineteen. It had a dozen divisions and took forty minutes. By trying to go everywhere, I failed to arrive anywhere. A good motto for the beginner is our national motto: "E pluribus unum." Too many speeches are like the man's hunting dog that chased everything in sight: there were "too many kinds of dog in him." Sidelights are irresistible to some minds. Too many points, too, leave an uncertain impression. The danger in expository preaching is in choosing a passage that contains more than one idea. Settle it with yourself beforehand which is the most important thing in your outline; and let neither fear of running out too soon nor special fondness for a particular division overstress a point that is secondary.

It is possible for a speaker to do justice to one idea. We sometimes hear the comment made on a speaker: "I can't remember the words that he used, but that speech changed my life." The speaker had chosen one idea, and driven it home. By clinging to one idea, you will compel your hearers to take a definite point of view regarding it, so that your point of view becomes theirs. The old rules of unity and coherence expressed with clearness and force, will never be outgrown, in any style of speaking. Carlyle: "I wish I could find the part again, this Speaking One; and stick to it with tenacity, with deadly energy, for there is need of him yet."

Progress is unity in development. The unity that has been emphasized is not like a crystal, but like a growing plant. It is organic, not mechanical. Our next question is: How can one idea, once presented, progress? In four ways.

First, there must be progress in interest. Avoid being too interesting in the introduction, as you avoid a dull one. Do not serve the dessert first. Save the most interesting thoughts and illustrations for the last. Work for climax. Some speeches are like skyrockets pointed into the ground, instead of culminating in a burst of glory in the sky. Your art, in this respect, is like that of the novelist. Study for their climacteric the two greatest stories in literature, *The Prodigal Son* and *The Good Samaritan*. There is no falling-off in the interest in the application. Like the law of nature that follows its children through seed, plant, blossom, to the fruit, so a good speaker mounts as he goes.

> "The best is yet to be,
> The last . . . for which the first was made."

The great historical addresses of St. Paul, Warren Hastings, Wm. J. Bryan, hold the hearers in suspense as their minds travel together from former days to the actions and decisions that the immediate present demands.

Second, to attain progress in interest, there must be progress in thought. Progress in thought from the simple to the complex. Your thought on any subject grows in width and depth as you pursue the central idea in your mind before putting pen to paper. Certain profound aspects of the subject flash into your mind as you proceed. Follow these out to their conclusion, and enter them in your analysis in cumulative order. Sheridan's ride would never have become famous if it had been made on a merry-go-round. As each thought is elaborated sufficiently to make sure that it is clear to the hearer, and so driven home that he will retain it, more valuable and profound thoughts will be expected and received by him in the logical chain of reasoning that carries speaker and hearer from height to height as they ascend in company. Every idea is necessary both to the one that precedes it and to the one that follows it.

Third: with progress in interest and progress in thought, the speech that wins attention will have progress in emotion. Save the things that move, that touch the heart, until the evolution of your thought is ready to use them. Let your audience feel the storm gathering. A congregation feels like Livingstone: "Lead me anywhere, so it be forward." Each step of the ascent should command a more glorious prospect. It is not enough to make an audience think. They are likely to think to little purpose unless they are stirred in soul. "Would you be a strong orator? Think deeply. A stirring orator? Feel deeply. An uplifting orator? Love deeply."

Fourth: it may be assumed that if there be progress in reflection and sensation, there will be progress in delivery. Advice to remember is to "start slow." Let your delivery take fire as you go along. Progress in delivery will include (a) the voice, in the two factors of volume and speed. It will involve progress (b) in facial expression, as a skillful actor shows in his features the growing earnestness of the drama in which he is engaged. (c) There will be also progress in gesture, like the parts of a machine responding to the push of inward power.

Brevity is the handmaid of both unity and progress. Phillips Brooks in his *Lectures on Preaching* emphasizes the man behind the sermon, but I would enter a plea for the man in front of the sermon. He too is the man that needs our sympathy. A habit that is assumed for a purpose, but achieves the opposite, may continue unnoticed for years unless one has a wise wife or is favored with an outspoken enemy. In the *Sermon on the Mount* the Master condemns overmuch speaking. So do the saints and the sinners in the pews. They want condensed worth in small packages. It is easier to carry away. Whitefield is said to have declared that there are no conversions after the first half hour. The Lacedemonians laid special emphasis on eliminating all non-essential parts of their speeches—perhaps partly because their audience was standing. It might be well to remove the pews from our churches. The editor of the *Ram's Horn* complained that many ministers, in preparing their sermons, prepared no place to stop.

There are four exceptions to the law of brevity: First, the literary or historical address which, not requiring concentrated thought, nor kindling strong emotions, may be listened to for some length of time without fatigue. Dr. Thomas Armitage of New York, an historical preacher, often spoke for an hour and a half. Second, where long illustrations are employed, like the legal illustrations which may bolster an important brief; and like "Billy" Sunday's biographical illustrations from his associates of the baseball diamond. Third, expository sermons, like those of Alexander Maclaren and G. Campbell Morgan. Fourth, dramatic speeches, like Charles M. Sheldon's chapters from his books, or like a play in the theater.

These exceptions apart, there is probably nothing against which the man on the street has a more incurable grudge than that of long speeches. "Only the short speaker is invited to return." People are more generous, except with the offering, in church than elsewhere, for while they will not tolerate short measure in percale or tobacco, when it comes to preaching they do not want too much for their money. The preacher, too, is different from men in other occupations, in that while everybody else is clamoring for shorter hours, he is determined to keep on when everybody wants him to stop. Audiences have changed greatly in this respect. Some one has called attention to the location of clocks. Formerly they were placed on the outside of the church, in order that the congregation might not be late; now they are on the inside, in order that the preacher may quit on time. Mahaffy, in his excellent book, *The Decay of Modern Preaching,* tells us of Bishop Burnet, who had an hour-glass standing on his pulpit desk. When the sand ran out, his hearers would frequently beg him to turn it other end up and go on for a second hour. I have heard of a church in our own day where grooves run from the pews, which hold boxes of marbles. When the hearer thinks the sermon should end, he drops a marble into a groove, and when marbles enough have accumulated, pulpit and preacher sink out of sight. John Haselbach, of the University of Vienna, in the good old days, gave a series of expositions from the book of *Isaiah.* After twenty years, he had not finished the first chapter. At that rate, it would have taken him one thousand three hundred and fifty years to complete the exposition. It is, of course, the quality rather than the quantity, or lack of it, which matters most. Your speech should not be too short merely for the sake of brevity.

The late Dr. Burdette, who charmed his great audiences in the Temple Church in Los Angeles, felt the utmost contempt for "fifteen-minute sermons," as if one could do justice to eternal truth in a quarter-hour. A small package is easily lost. You must make your point and drive it home. But, if you are a young speaker, it is better to err on the side of brevity and test yourself and your hearers. When you get older, you can lengthen your speeches as it seems necessary—and safe. By that time you will have formed the habit of conciseness and unity. Never speak till your audience grows restless. You may be speaking from a platform as a visitor, where the audience have been trained to listen to short speeches, and they will give you their attention longer than they ought to because they are expecting you to stop. A farmer's wife told me the other day that she gave her chickens food only twice a day, and then only as much as they would eat clean. Feed the hearer and leave him hungry for more. Sermons should imitate Enoch, by walking with God, and not Methuselah, who was famous only for the length of his life. The man that kept on preaching until only one auditor remained said that he "hated to stop as long as there was any-one that wanted to hear the gospel."

The reason for over-long addresses is usually that they are dull, and the speaker keeps on in the hope of hitting on something interesting. He is looking for a good place to stop, like picnickers in the woods. A short address takes proportionately longer to prepare than a long one. The less a man has to say, the longer it takes him to say it. Muddy water settles slowly. George Eliot: "Empty wagons rattle prodigiously." The short address requires not only preparation, but elimination. Excrescences, irrelevant material, overelaboration, must be pruned. Warmth requires less clothing than does frigidity. A gem-cutter has to be more skillful than a quarryman. Ideas that have not been made transparent in the study must be clarified on the platform. A reputation for stopping when one is through is a valuable asset. It is like credit in the commercial world. People will not follow the guide that has lost the way. Fortunate is he of whom it may be repeated what Ben Jonson said of a popular speaker: "The fear of every man that heard him was lest he should make an end."

The cure is easy—stop talking and sit down. If you ask, "Will this not make an anti-climax?"—the worst anti-climax is to lose the ears of your hearers. Introduce your closing sentence. Let

> "silence like a poultice come
> To heal the blows of sound."

Give the audience some intimation that your speech is near its end, and then stand by the intimation. The question may be asked: "How can I know how long I have spoken?" You can lay your watch on the lectern, and in time you will cultivate a sense of the length of time you have been talking, and hardly vary a moment from your estimate. Some sleepers can wake themselves up in the morning without an alarm-clock. Most speakers have no such consciousness, and underestimate the flight of time. Young speakers almost invariably prepare too much material, through the dread of not having enough. These are splendid words of J. M. Buckley:

> "The whole art of making a speech is to have something pertinent and moving to say, to say something all the time, to say it vivaciously; if it is a religious speech, to say it with religious feeling; and to stop when every one wants you to go on."

16

EXTEMPORE SPEAKING

In ancient Athens, among the various objects of worship, the Greeks built an altar to Rumor: their high intelligence reverenced the circulation of ideas by speech. The tongue of one whale will yield a ton of oil. The tongue of Wm. J. Bryan yielded, I suppose, five hundred dollars a night. The tongue of John Wesley yielded the Methodist denomination, with over sixteen millions of followers in the United States. The tongue, though so profitable to the man that knows how to wield it, is a comparatively inexpensive piece of machinery. It never requires oiling; does not rust or wear thin; can easily be carried about; does not have to be set up in each new location; and occupies surprisingly little space for the amazing products it throws off. For its varied uses, the speaker finds four methods in which the speech may be prepared and delivered. He is at liberty to choose any one of the four, but once having chosen it as his method he will not be likely to find it easy to use more than one of these methods habitually, nor to change from one to another at will, without making the change permanent.

First, you can read from manuscript. That is, you can write out your address in full, and read it verbatim, as you would if it were the work of another author. You are at liberty, in this case, to add thoughts that are suggested to you as you read, and to incorporate your illustrations and quotations as you like. If you do this, however, you are in danger of over-stepping your time limit. Reading from manuscript is the old-time method, when all audiences with few exceptions expected a manuscript, and were a bit suspicious of the honest labor of any other speaker. My father, who was pastor of the largest Protestant church in

Connecticut for twenty-nine years, always read his sermons, had crowded houses, and many accessions to the membership. Reading from manuscript appears to have been "Billy" Sunday's method, though he knew his sermons so well that he rarely needed to refer to his notes. There are advantages in this method. The speaker can say exactly what he wants to say. In case of being misunderstood, or being deliberately misquoted by a malignant newspaper, he can verify what he has said, for he has it down in black and white. He can use more elegant English, be more accurate in his facts, and he can regulate the length of his speech. When the visiting Scotchman, in the warmth of his enthusiasm, said: "I could go on and on—" an aged dame in the gallery called out: "Nay, ye couldna: ye've only ane page left." Reading frees a young speaker from stage-fright, and all worry as to what he is to say: the game is already in the bag. It affords you protection against a cold mood, and against anti-climax, either of which, from a variety of causes, threatens every speaker. Your notes are in a form to be preserved, unless rats, fire, or flood destroy them. Such a manuscript is ready for publication. Every speaker knows how a reporter may call immediately after his address, or telephone for a digest of it just before he goes to the platform; and with his manuscript carefully written out, he can oblige him and extend his own influence through the papers.

There are disadvantages in reading. The preparation is laborious, too laborious for a busy man, and takes so much time that a sudden demand cannot be met. It tends to make you a slave to words, fastening your attention too closely on forms of expression. It rouses the suspicion of the audience, who have a strong distaste for anything "cut and dried." When they see a speaker draw out his manuscript, they heave a deep "Now-we're-in-for-it" sigh. As one somewhat sophistically: "If he can't remember what he's going to say, how can he expect us to?" During the war if one of the hut-speakers produced a manuscript, as soon as he happened to raise his eyes from it he would find that half of his audience had silently stolen away. It was the only occasion on which American soldiers beat a retreat. Beecher: "A written sermon is apt to reach out to people like a gloved hand; an unwritten sermon reaches out the warm and glowing palm, bared to the touch."

The written discourse does not readily adjust itself to conditions. It has not the flexibility to meet the mood of an audience, nor to fit the mood of the speaker himself. It cannot receive and use the inspiration that is "blown to him from the seats." It fetters and confines your speech like a hard mould. Your eyes and mind cannot catch enough of it at a glance to make you independent. You have to keep looking down: "Be good and you'll be—oh, yes, happy!" "There's many a slip 'twixt the cup and the sauc— Oh, no, lip." John Selden, a great British scholar of the seventeenth century, wrote in Greek in every book in his library: "Above all, liberty!" He felt perhaps that anything that is already written down is a menace to mental freedom. Reading limits dramatic action. If one attempts gestures at all while reading, his motions are like those of a man swimming: they have to be made above the surface of his desk. The reading habit is liable to become a crutch, from whose support the user can hardly break away without halting. Your notes, so carefully prepared and preserved, are liable to be used on future occasions without revision when, though not quite appropriate to the new occasion, there is the temptation to make them fit. It gives their possessor the feeling that they are "all done"; and, as one has said, we are all as lazy as we dare to be.

There are occasions for reading from manuscript, when no other device is so good. There are times when it is important to speak carefully, to choose one's words, as in time of self-defence against critics, on trial, or in controversy. If you are to deliver an address on a scientific subject, or technical, before special groups, you are safer from embarrassing misstatements if armed with a manuscript. Many such groups expect a paper, as a matter of course; though "paper" is frequently a conventional name for any carefully prepared talk.

A hint or two as to the use of a manuscript will be in place here. Let the writing be large and distinct enough to be read easily in poor light. If there is a chorus gallery behind your platform, the chorister is quite likely to turn out the lights above you, especially if there are members of his chorus engaged to be married—and there usually are. It is necessary to become thoroughly familiar with your manuscript, the work of preparation having only fairly begun with the writing of the last word. Take time for preparation, and practice on delivery. It must not be forgotten that it is much more difficult to interest an audience with full notes, and to hold their attention even after you have won it. Manuscript addresses need concrete illustration, vivid gesticulation, variety of tone color, in fact all the enlivening features that can stir an audience. A plain face needs a handsome hat. When the spirit is on fire, and painstaking preparation has been made, manuscripts do not seem to be tanglefoots. Dr. Chalmers, Edinburgh's famous civic preacher, we are told, always used an old-fashioned manuscript in a marvel of fine print writing; but one day being stirred beyond his wont he forgot his notes, stormed up and down the platform, thundering his denunciations of public sin in a frenzy of earnestness, until his hearers also forgot where they were, and a man rose and shouted: "Good for you, Chalmers!" If you're that kind, stick to your manuscript.

Second, the memoriter method, as it is called, goes a step farther and not only writes in full, but commits the whole manuscript to memory, and recites it. A brother of mine, who has the most extraordinary memory I know, seems to experience little difficulty in speaking memoriter. This method has all the advantages of reading, and in addition enables the speaker to look his audience in the eye all the time; to move about, if he wish to; to gesticulate naturally and not like an umbrella pine; and if delivered ingenuously the memorized address gives its user the appearance of being a polished and finished speaker, with the language of a written production while apparently speaking off-hand. To address an audience memoriter is the highest compliment you can pay them, except that it does not allow for the inspiration that comes from them in extempore address. It strengthens the memory which, like a growing giant, carries with increasing ease larger and larger loads.

The disadvantages of this method are obvious. It is the most laborious of all methods, taking the double time and toll of writing in full on paper, and then transcribing the whole to the tablets of the brain cells. Suppose you average one address a day? This method, adopted to avoid stage-fright, really tends to bring it on. If you lose a link in your chain or, what is worse, think you may, you are stalled. The memoriter speaker usually has an unnatural manner. The faraway gaze at the mental picture of the manuscript gives a glassy look to the eye, as of one who looks at his audience without seeing them. He can hardly achieve adjustment to his environment, for he is tethered to his unseen manuscript. The method is impracticable for impromptu occasions, unless your memory is stored with a varied selection of original paragraphs, all at your tongue's end for such calls. Your memory must be so flexible, your hold on your notes so secure and yet so light, that you can go on smoothly if you forget here and there; or can change, if a sudden inspiration flashes upon you, or some unforeseen event crashes into your environment. But, to mingle the matter cast in a mould and the effervescing fancies of the moment is like mixing oil and water.

The memoriter method may be modified by writing the beginning and end of your speech, only, and learning these. John Bright of England usually wrote out the concluding words and sentences, as being the most important for his auditors to remember. If these parts are read, however, they call your eyes to the paper when there is most need to look at your audience. If memorized, they impart the constraint attached to that method.

Third, the extempore style of speaking is best for most persons in this day. By extemporary speaking is not meant speaking without any preparation. It is an optimism amounting to infatuation to imagine that you can make an acceptable speech without any preparation. There is nothing to be said in its favor. It is like trying to read aloud a ten-page essay out of a blank book. There is never an occasion when it is necessary to speak with no preparation. It may happen, you object, that one is called upon to speak when he did not expect it. But you should not get into such a predicament. "How can I avoid it?" (a) Before starting for a place where you are not invited to be a speaker, but have reason to think there may be several short speeches, prepare against such a contingency as being asked to replace someone that is absent, or to add a word to what others have said, by having ready a few thoughts and illustrations. It is better to carry an umbrella when it fails to rain than to get soaked for want of something to put up in time of need. (b) When you are in a public gathering, where you supposed there was to be no speaking, and it begins, set your wits to working and think out something, so that if you happen to be called on you will at least have a respectable start, a point of embarkation. (c) If, in such a case, you are the first one called on, as out of a clear sky? Be ready at all times by having in your memory kitbag a few entertaining or inspiring things that will do for any occasion. These will help you to hoist your sails, and perhaps the breeze from heaven will catch them. (d) If you cannot say anything worth while, there is always one dignified course open to you: you can decline to speak. Don't insult your audience, and ruin your reputation as a man or woman of sense, if not of talent, by emitting vacuous insipidities. An audience has little charity for the vanity of striving after wind by a man that imagines that what has no interest for himself may look amusing or kindle thought in another. It doesn't work that way. One speaker of whom I heard resorted to an ingenious way out. When asked for his address, when he had not expected to be called upon, he rose and said: "My address is 23 Euclid Avenue: I shall be happy to have you call to see me," and sat down. If one does not find the way in, why not take the way out?

Extemporary speaking, in its present definition, is speaking without fully written manuscript. It has strong advantages. It can be adapted to circumstances. We all feel like the young speaker: "Whenever I read my address, I am easy until I speak, and then I am in misery; when I speak extempore, I am in misery until I begin to speak, and then I am happy." It is a delight to open your thought, and find expression for it, when on the platform. If not hampered with manuscript, there is room for the play of passion, as it is enkindled by the responsive eager faces before you. An arctic explorer whom I heard in Boston said that his ice hut had inside a temperature of one hundred and forty degrees below zero; but that every native that came in raised it ten degrees: "To raise the temperature, add an Eskimo." That is what the public speaker finds to be true of a spiritual and mental temperature. His best thoughts often occur to him while speaking. He is unencumbered by a pile of pages. There is frequently no place to put them. They are conspicuous. You feel as if you had let strangers come behind your counter, into your private workshop.

An extempore speaker can rearrange the divisions, if he find them illogical during delivery. In the application of close thinking, he forgets himself and his appearance. The unwritten speech tends to create a natural feeling, as in conversation between friends. It is easier to revise for the next occasion. Acquiring proficiency, the work of speaking grows easier and easier. Then, as Defoe: "Attempting to teach others is sometimes the best way of teaching ourselves"; you are soon glad to discover that the effort of helping your hearers with their problems, in a frank, unaffected way, has helped you to the mastery of your own dreaded task.

If you bring a page of notes to the lectern, let it be written in clear distinct lettering. Black ink is better than type-writing for your purpose, because you can make larger letters, and can vary its appearance in a way to catch the eye instantly at a glance. Dr. James L. Gordon, a popular preacher, formerly of San Francisco, used a number of pages, with comparatively few lines to a page, in large characters, visible at several steps from his desk. Take time to become familiar with your analysis. You will find that it takes about as long to familiarize yourself with the page of notes that you take in with you for reference, as it does to commit the whole outline to memory, a twenty-minute speech requiring about an hour and a half after it has previously been written. Know it so well that you will not be chained to it like *Prometheus Bound*. Do not pore over it so long that it grows stale. Do not make your analysis too full. There is a tendency to write more and more fully, which must be striven against. A naturally fluent speaker needs but ten or a dozen clauses; but a more reticent man will need more. A few catch-words or heads written out are less of a strain on the memory than a memorized analysis, and allow the speaker almost as much freedom. Such a brief takes but little space to preserve. Several dozen may be carried on the train in a speaking tour. When the analysis has thus been made, give it long and concentrated thought. John Bright would sometimes think out his analyses while lying abed. We have the picture of Wendell Phillips, stretched on his lounge, thinking out his plan, trusting to filling it in when on his feet, where his tried experience would draw at will "upon his vast accumulated store of facts and illustrations."

Fourth, there are some reasons why the best method of all may be to speak without notes. A biographer of Phillips says that he spoke almost always without notes; and that on the few occasions when he did use them, they were an evident embarrassment: "It was like an eagle walking." But perhaps this is only emphasizing the truth that it is difficult to change from one method to another. However, it is easier for an eagle to walk, than for a tortoise to try to fly. There are decided advantages in extempore speaking wholly without notes. The impression on the audience is distinctly favorable. They feel that you are talking to them face to face, that you have complete command of the situation, your ease giving them ease. Dr. Baldwin said, "In a speech an occasional abruptness or hesitation or looseness of language may be readily passed over." You have no notes to carry in your pocket; or, worse still, to forget and leave at home. You do not need to step frequently to the lectern to consult them, which is a slight drawback (in both a figurative and a literal sense), when you have found yourself, in the heat of your argument, at another part of the platform. If it gives you more freedom, you can dispense altogether with the lectern table, which is always a barrier between you and your audience. You are not embarrassed when there is no table or desk available.

Speaking quite without notes is a tonic to the memory, and training and concentration of mind both in preparation and in delivery. The speaker forms a picture in his mind of the written page, with the location of each division and subdivision, as if it lay before him in sight. It is the ability to do this that makes the good speller, or accountant. Remembering was difficult for me in school. I tried two methods without success: reading the history lesson rapidly a dozen times; then slowly and carefully the paragraph. I learned the secret of concentration in the following way: with watch before me, I read a paragraph with close attention; then closing the book tried to see how much I remembered. Referring to the book, I added the second time what had been forgotten in the first; and when that paragraph was mastered, took the second in the same manner, and then went back and reviewed both. I found my memory to be as good as anybody's. I have gone into this matter in detail, for I am convinced that many beginners in extempore speaking have a similar struggle. The joy of mastery is possible to every one; and the memory grows amazingly by exercise. The extempore speaker comes to have much of the grace of expression of the memoriter method, verbatim quotations and groups of figures presenting few terrors for him.

The objections to using no notes: (1) It is an unnecessary burden on the memory, a single page of analysis bringing, as I have already pointed out, almost as much freedom, though not quite. (2) There is not always time to memorize the analysis, and to adopt a new method is awkward. (3) An excellent plan, for the first few years, is to write out an occasional address in full; then lay it aside, and use an analysis. But be careful not to try to recall the words themselves. Uncouthness of expression will be discovered and overcome when one attempts to put one's thoughts in writing. Your vocabulary will be enlarged, and a grace of style cultivated that will have its after-effect on extempore addresses. An art so difficult to learn as public speech, and one that so gloriously rewards its devotees, is worth taking pains about. Make up your mind that what others have done you can do. If you do it as well as you can, you will not be responsible for doing it as well as they can.

17

AFTER-DINNER SPEAKING
AND LECTURING

There is an eternal variety about speaking in public. Each kind is so different from the others, that it constitutes almost a different profession. Wrote Terence, the Latin poet: "I take it to be a principal rule of life not to be too much addicted to any one thing." There is no danger, as far as the orator is concerned! Turning over a page or two of his index of addresses, the average minister may find that they include speeches to old folk, boys and girls, on the ocean (when I finished the congregation were at sea), Socialists, South Sea Islanders, Salvation Army, Red Cross, fraternal orders, Y.W.C.A., Rotary Club, Y.M.C.A., revival meetings, Thanksgiving, the Grange, prison, women's clubs, undertakers, birthday social, insurance companies, lawyers and judges, picnics, corner-stone laying, college athletic rallies, soldiers' barracks, hospitals, high schools, theological seminaries, and what not. A speaker's audience varies.

The usual discourse of twenty or thirty minutes' length before the average audience I have already discussed. In this chapter we shall consider the special problems of two kinds of addresses, namely, after-dinner speaking and the lecture.

The after-dinner speech may be a conventional set address or popular lecture delivered to the guests at table. Such a discourse comes under the general treatment already given. The typical Chauncey M. Depew type of after-dinner speech is in a class by itself, and presents problems not met anywhere else. It is one of the easiest speeches in the world for a man of the right temperament, and one of the most formidable for everybody else. Often it is a lugubrious failure. While the average man or woman can not and need not look for brilliant effects, such as scintillate from the brain of a Chesterton or a Will Rogers (sometimes), yet by observing certain essentials of the art, he may carry on with credit to himself and pleasure to his hearers. There are two distinct parts to consider.

THE TOASTMASTER

A brief experience in this part is long enough to show that little details have a lot to do with the happiness or discomfort of the evening. First, the toastmaster should see that the meal is served promptly. Misunderstanding in this matter may lead to a deal of confusion. Do not introduce speakers during the removal of dishes after a course has been served. Let the business parts of the program, or the band numbers, take place at these times. A banquet, run at loose ends, may easily last from six o'clock till nine-thirty, everybody gets tired out before the program begins, and nobody knows what's the matter. The question of good ventilation, such as to secure fresh air without draughts, deserves study.

Have the program in your hands hours beforehand. When possible, arrange the order of it yourself, or have a hand in its arrangement, so as to secure both variety and climax, and see that there is something doing that is interesting every moment of the program-time. Let the solos, recitation, stunts, toasts, or whatever is provided, blend in a lively and constructive way. The president of the organization before which you introduce the speakers will first present you as the toastmaster, though not always. Then, if time permits, you may appropriately give a ten minutes' speech, by way of launching the program. You are to offer some valuable contribution to the thought of the evening. No speech must be made under any circumstances that does not actually "get somewhere." When the minister remarked to the barber that he was to supply the local pulpit for a month, the barber, who had not before heard that term, asked: "Supply it with what?" What, indeed?

Prepare an introduction for each feature of the program. You must mellow up your crowd, and create a happy atmosphere. These introductions must be exceedingly brief, and varied, and not all fun. Remember Prof. Talcott's warning: "It is easier to make an average audience weep than to make it laugh." While most of your introductions may be amusing, some of them eulogistic of the coming speaker or musician, let none of them be cheap or commonplace. Have one story noted on the side of your private program for each speaker, or a thought on his subject, or a quip. Have a half dozen extra ones at the bottom of the page for following speakers, if necessary, replying to a "slam" on their part, or for introductions to unexpected additions to the program, or to connect the preceding with the following speaker. When David went to meet Goliath he took with him five smooth pebbles, though he needed but one. Keep the atmosphere happy, and social. Wait a moment, while you ask them to turn their chairs so as to face the speakers' table. This will prevent a good deal of subsequent scuffing.

THE TOASTS

If you are one of the speakers called upon by the toastmaster, take your stand when you rise to speak where you can face everybody, if possible. It is important, after a big dinner, to get everybody's eye. If they are tired by the time your turn comes to speak, you can rest them by some simple device, like asking them to rise and give three cheers for somebody. Make your talk short. James Russell Lowell prescribed that an after-dinner talk should contain a platitude, an anecdote, and then quit. Begin: "Mr. Toastmaster, ladies and gentlemen." If he has been hard on you, you may begin, "Mr. Roastmaster." If there are many ministers in your audience, you can begin: "Men, women, and ministers." That is, start with a happy and amusing introduction; but do not feel that under all circumstances the first sentence must be an attempt to be funny. If all tragedy were taken out of the world, it would return at the striving of serious men to be cute. Nothing else takes like local hits. The minstrels have taught us that. In trying for a local hit, one need not be like the British clergyman who, in traveling, began each address: " Dear Edinburgh souls," "Dear Manchester souls," and—"Dear Cork souls." Your local reference may be to your introducer, the program, the weather, the dinner, the guests, etc. Remember that audiences delight in good-natured abuse. A toastmaster may say that in Colorado the climate is so perfect that it is said no one dies: they only dry up and blow away; but here, it seems to be the opposite; they blow away, but they never dry up. Such horseplay generally "goes" with banqueters. Sam Jones, the Southern evangelist, advised Dr. Brougher, of Oakland: "Skin a man, and smile while you're skinning him, and he'll follow you to the tannery for the hide."

If you use notes, do not type-write them, unless they are on cards to be held in your hand. Typing is too small and too difficult of distinctive emphasis, to be laid on a table before you, where the lights are remote or too dim to see them plainly. Do not hold them in your hand, if you can see them from the table.

Make one really worth while point in your speech. All chaff makes a poor harvest. Strange to say, "the narrower the subject, the easier the treatment"; a hold-back strap is easier to discuss than a harness; patriotism than internationalism. Choose when you can the topic that is dear to you. You will be more likely to give it the earnest backing it deserves, if you handle a favorite theme. Get somewhere. All's well that ends well. Make brain and heart go together. Interest and entertain yourself, and you will entertain your fellow diners.

THE LECTURE

The platform lecture differs from the ordinary address: first, in length, lasting from fifty minutes to two hours, the average being an hour and fifteen minutes. Its length has a bearing upon its character. Second, it is a money-making institution. However useful it may be to the audience, neither they nor the speaker forget, or ought to, that he is to be paid for it. Third, it is delivered to a special audience, a lecture audience.

The successful lecture, whether on a Chautauqua platform or in the college classroom, will be distinguished by three things. It will be entertaining, holding the interest from introduction to climax. It should furnish practical advice on the problems of life. The student should make a study of Conwell's *Acres of Diamonds,* asking himself what are the features that have given it its immense popularity. We are all conscious of need, and instinctively cultivate those that can help us, and we keep coming back to them for more. The successful lecture will also contain novel information, information that is not to be found else-

where. A lecture may be prepared to serve any one of the three
ends I have mentioned: it may entertain, advise, or instruct;
or do all three. It is best delivered without notes, except on informal occasions, or in the classroom, where a written digest is
fitting.

The lectures most in demand are those by specialists in air
navigation, literary criticism, archaeology, health discoveries,
deep-sea diving, scientific invention, and the like, men that have
learned or done something unique, something of public value.
If physicians were not generally poor speakers, they could command splendid returns from their knowledge of the care of the
human body. People want to learn things from their lecturers.
A good humorous lecture is in great demand, but humor is the
rarest of all intellectual gifts. Men of eloquence can get a good
hearing, no matter what they discuss; for, like the sun, they never
touch anything without illuminating it. Wm. Jennings Bryan,
Lady Astor, Thomas Dixon, Jr., "Bob" Burdette, Bernard Shaw,
have never disappointed their audiences.

For the man without native genius, but who is willing to work
hard, and is possessed of good natural intelligence, the surest
center-fire subject is efficiency. Effective subjects for the efficiency
lecture are: work, poor boys that have made good, optimism,
patience, perseverance, self-reliance, self-education, knowledge of
men, enthusiasm, married life, initiative, thinking, thrift, sympathy, pluck, will, strength, courage, health, conversation, making
the most of what you have, ambition, success. With taking titles,
and handled in an inspiring way, one or more of these topics finds
the door to the ear. Give your chosen subject long and painstaking study. An immense amount of thought and investigation is essential if the lecture is to bear up on a circuit. Preparation may take a year or two. *Ecclesiasticus:* "He that de-
spiseth small things shall fall little by little." "Milton conceived
Paradise Lost at thirty-two, but didn't compose it till after twenty
years of further preparation." The "Stetson Law," established
a few years ago in California, sends those that refuse to work to
the penitentiary. It ought to apply to public lecturers.

Pay the price. Your lecture ought to cost you more than it does
the public. An Italian journalist to the Grand Vizier of Turkey:
"Would your highness consent to the sale of Crete?" "Certainly,

any one can have it at the price we paid for it—twenty years'
war."

> "Supposin' fish don't bite at first,
>   What are you goin' to do?
> Throw down your pole, chuck out your bait,
>   An' say your fishin's through?
> You bet you ain't: you're goin' to fish,
>   An' fish, an' fish, an' wait
> Until you've ketched a basketful
>   Or used up all your bait.
>
> "Suppose success don't come at first,
>   What are you goin' to do?
> Throw up the sponge and kick yourself?
>   An' growl, an' fret, an' stew?
> You bet you ain't, you're goin' to fish,
>   An' bait an' bait agin,
> Until success will bite your hook,
>   For grit is sure to win."

18

GESTICULATION AND DRAMATIC ACTION

The object of gesture in speaking is not to "let off steam," or for the purpose of display, as some of its critics seem to assume, but to deepen the impression made by the spoken word: in the last analysis, to improve the status of those that listen, to "wave the hand, that they may enter the gates of the nobles." Watkins: "The words we utter are only part of what we really say." In old John Bunyan's *Holy War*, when Prince Immanuel fought to win Mansoul, we are told that he besieged all five gates, that is, he appealed to all the five senses. Most speakers attack only one—Ear Gate. The present chapter proposes plans for besieging also Eye Gate. "People in large crowds hear best with the eye." Xanthes, an ancient Greek authority on speaking in public: "Speakers who are contented just to speak do not take long to weary those that hear them." Gesture and bodily animation come naturally in the street-corner argument. The speaker must learn to let them come as naturally on the platform.

For freedom of movement, dress comfortably. The height of fashion sometimes leads to the depths of discomfort. Assume a natural position on the platform. Stand firmly on both feet, keeping your weight placed forward on the balls of the feet. Weight on the heels deadens the whole body. Do not let your feet get separated, like those of a calf learning to walk. Walk naturally, avoiding both the stiffness which moves by hitches and budges, and the over-ease that slouches. A speaker at ease, expressing grace and dignity, puts an audience at ease. Xanthes: "An orator should never forget that he will be judged by his attitude. He presents himself before speaking, and if his pose displease the public, he will have a thousand times more difficulty in winning its favor." The athletic man will have little occasion to study his poses.

Gestures are to speech what pictures are to a book. Always precede the word by the gesture, starting the arm a split second before the thought which it illustrates. In such an expression as, "The bird flew away," before the words are spoken they are prepared for by the hand and arm first, unfolding them like a moving paint-brush. There are two main types of gesture, somewhat clearly demarcated, perhaps best designated as descriptive and conceptive. Esenwein illustrates how the fist may be used for each type: "The fist gesture represents that which is *forcible* in its character, addressing itself to the *will;* when used descriptively, it represents that which *grasps, confines,* or *controls.*"

Descriptive gestures are those illustrating material objects, or space. "They serve to designate form, movement, dimension, situation." Another author: "How truly language must be regarded as a hindrance to thought, though the necessary instrument of it, we shall clearly perceive on remembering the comparative force with which simple ideas are communicated by signs. To say, 'Leave the room,' is less expressive than to point to the door. Placing the finger on the lips is more forcible than whispering, 'Do not speak.' A beck of the hand is better than 'Come here.' No phrase can convey the idea of surprise so vividly as opening the eyes and raising the eyebrows. A shrug of the shoulders would lose much by translation into words."

Elocutionists used to teach a carefully planned scheme of rules governing gesture, indicating how to hold the arm for fear, anger, grief, etc. Most of these systems have now been abandoned. In their place has come the single admonition that the really bad gesture is only the one which calls attention to itself instead of to the idea it is meant to enliven. Let the arm be used from the shoulder, let the elbows be free from the body, and let the thumb be kept inconspicuous; for the rest, gesture as the inclination comes.

Conceptive gestures, or gestures of impression, as they are sometimes called, are used to emphasize an idea by suggesting the spiritual, rather than the material, concept. Gestures made with the arm are naturally more ample in the open air than when made in a room. The arms are spread in addressing a large company. Never make a gesture from the elbow, or from the wrist; but use the whole arm, with freedom of movement. Watkins warns high school students to get the wrist loose, some speakers using "the hand and forearm as if it were one long, straight rod." The wrist-movements taught by the golf-instructor exhibit the necessary flexibility. Timidity has a tendency to make one hold the elbow back, making spurts of "undeveloped awkwardness," like a chicken with its wings clipped trying to fly. With regard to the hand, it should generally be flat and open, the thumb not tucked in, the fingers close, but not touching one another. Do not stand like a grandfather clock with your hands before your face; nor suffer your hands to interfere with each other. Every shrinking, curled, half-made gesture indicates fear of the audience, the hands held "as if you had bird-shot in each hollow, and feared it would roll out."

Though easy and natural, the speaker is to be self-restrained, his gestures being limited in number and in emotional expression. The story is familiar, of Voltaire, preparing a young actress to appear in one of his tragedies, tying her hands to her side with thread, to check her tendency to over-gesticulation. At the beginning, she moved forward into her recitation with calmness; but at length, carried away with her feelings, she threw her hands into the air, breaking the packthreads. Somewhat ashamed of having thus broken her bounds, she apologized for it; but Voltaire, smiling: "I intended you to break the fastening threads, when your enthusiasm made it irresistible." Such gestures as you make must be in harmony with the tenor of your address, and the nature of the thought you are expressing.

To gesture every sentence, like a Southern fiery speaker whom I heard recently in San Francisco, gives the impression of want of poise. Let your introduction proceed for some time without visual accompaniment. Nor let your gestures be too fast and furious. A speaker whose appearance resembles that of Kwannon, the Oriental goddess of Mercy with her six arms, only confuses his hearers, turning auditors into spectators. Even in the heat of a financial campaign, it should be remembered that a windmill is not intended to "raise the wind." Let gesticulation be always dignified, its whole purpose being to clarify and impress your idea. The character of the audience, too, has its bearing, many more gestures being necessary before an audience of children, or unlearned persons, than before the average assembly.

The careful student of gesture will seek a pleasing variety, using now the right hand, now the left, thus including all of his audience. When not in use, let your hands hang naturally by your side, not with awkward stiffness like toothpicks stuck into a potato. Don't overwork the "hold-up" gesture, pointing with your finger at the audience, a favorite for some reason with beginners. Audiences prefer persuasion to dictation. "The repetition at regular intervals of the same gesture imparts restlessness to the listener who, in spite of himself, awaits and fears the repetition."

Gracefulness of carriage, if not innate, may be cultivated, as every observer of the military recruit, the dancing school, and the transformation between college freshman and senior years, knows. To acquire the habit of carrying yourself erect, it is necessary only to hold the head high, and your body will follow. When walking, imagine you are looking over a fence. The Orientals have won their proud poise of head and shoulders by the custom of carrying burdens on their heads. To balance a tall slender jar filled with water makes it necessary to stand like a mountain pine. Get athletic grace by athletic exercises. Eliminate all awkward positions when in private, or in social converse, such as arms a-kimbo, or awesomely folded, or clasped across the chest like the corpse of Tutankhamen, or grasping the abdomen like the Indian god-of-pain.

Develop force of character in order to become forceful on the platform. In forceful utterance, too much grace may appear effeminate. Strength is not awkward. The sculptured figures of Scopas and Praxiteles are illustrations of that. The statuary of the mid-Victorian period attained a grace that was effeminate, disappointing to the simpler taste of our day. *The Thinker* appears under Rodin's chisel as a muscular giant. Tenderness is possible only to strength. Limp and lax gestures, like an empty glove hung on the end of a poker, do not further an appeal to arms, except as enlisted against the creature that wields them. Twenty-five of the best known pastors in Chicago, says the United

Press, under the instructions of the physical director of the Chicago Y.M.C.A., are now going every week through all of the gymnastic exercises, in order "to fit themselves for their duties in the pulpit." A young minister no longer begins his pulpit ministrations with a "maiden effort."

The unreasoning objection to all rules about gesticulation is that it would be impossible to fasten the mind on such things without ruining one's speech, to which, of course, the answer is that gesticulation is to be learned by practice in private, and in the less emotional parts of one's speeches, until it becomes spontaneous. Practice before a mirror. The student will find an excellent discussion of this whole question in Woolbert's *The Fundamentals of Speech,* pages 124–142, which I would recommend for further study on the part of anyone who may wish to pursue the subject in greater detail. Emphasizing the necessity for diligent study, Woolbert: "Every man is just enough like the rabbit or the robin, so that when he is greatly frightened his first impulse is to 'freeze,' to make no motion that will attract attention."

The need for the use of the dramatic art in speaking is based on the truth of the old proverb: "Actions speak louder than words." Prof. Rollo Anson Tallcott: "The man who wishes to use his powers of expression in a practical way, as a lawyer, teacher, or salesman, can have no better preparation than a course in *acting* followed by one in public reading, taking them up in a more general way than his course in public speaking." Objections that are made to dramatic action on the speaker's part, and especially to its use in the pulpit, are based on the assumption that because the actor is playing the part of another, such action is insincere. Why so? Everything we do we have picked up by imitation. Our facial expressions, the words we speak, our quotations from literature, are not our own, but have been borrowed from outside. To convey a thought by the employment of such actions as would be used for its conveyance anywhere off the platform, is to convey it naturally, as the speaker uses tone colors that are associated with the conveyance of such ideas elsewhere. Action is but a figure of speech expressed by the body instead of only by the lips. The very fact that dramatic speakers, like the late T. DeWitt Talmage, draw the throngs that less vivid speakers seek for in vain, is evidence that the public in general like and will attend to the thing they malign. Dramatic action draws the people, because they like to see what they hear. "Did preachers labor to acquire a masterly *delivery*, places of public instruction would be crowded, as places of public diversion are now."

Dramatic action is to be differentiated from gesture, as being more comprehensive, including as it does the whole body. It presents the complete picture, like a book-illustration. When you accompany by appropriate action your account of stamping out a fire, reeling from a blow, laughing boisterously, dying, you are using the art of drama. "If we are suffering from fatigue, we stretch our arms; during great heat, we wipe the forehead; in headache, the hands go to the forehead; we dry our tears, etc." Dramatists have taught us that with practice all of these actions can be performed realistically without necessarily feeling the accompanying emotions. But, as will be noted later, the absence of genuine feeling, or the least bit of insincerity, will be instantly felt in the audience, and will cost the speaker much of his effectiveness. It was the opinion of Aristotle that the most effective element in persuasion was the audience' impression of the character of the speaker.

Dramatic action, it is evident, requires special study in addition to the study of one's notes. Observe men and women in their every-day activities, to learn how they act in various moods and conditions. Seek opportunities to observe actors on the legitimate stage. Watch the deaf in their expressive pantomime; make study of the moving-picture stars; attend the services of dramatic preachers. I remember to this day how the Rev. Emory J. Haynes in a sermon in a thronged New England church illustrated the text: "Doth he not count all my steps?" We were made to see the father at one end of the platform, watching his child as it left the mother's knee learning to walk, and how we shared her excitement, as she counted: "One—two—three—catch him, John!—four—five,—there!" That thorough-paced veteran in the dramatic art made that verse in *Job* live for me for a lifetime. Read with attention the biographies of famous actors, Edwin Booth and Garrett, Whitefield, the great Welsh preachers, Sarah Bernhardt. John B. Gough lifted the then-unpopular cause of temperance into public favor by his lectures, whose dramatic illustrations were drawn from his own past. Could any spellbound listener ever forget the two drunkards that took turns trying to take each other home in the wheelbarrow; how they careened from side to side, spilled each other out, finding the width of the road longer than the length of it? Or that husband whom the orator pictured seizing in the front hall the pitcher of water, not noticing a spool of thread that had dropped in it until it began to tickle his throat: he drew it out, hand over hand, before our fascinated eyes, and at length cried to his wife: "Maria! come down quick! I'm unravelin'!" No wonder that one of his hearers spoke of Gough as "the man that could lecture with his coattails"! His whole being was one animated discourse. The immense effectiveness of such proficiency is possible only to patient practice. The student that is not content with practice must be content with failure. For him, it is either hearse or rehearse. To those exceptious souls that say: "Talk is cheap: you must practice what you preach," we agree: and add that the practicing must be done beforehand.

It is even more true of acting than of gesture that it is to be used with moderation. No better rule for both has been given than Hamlet's to his players: "Suit the action to the word, the word to the action." In referring to physical objects, it is not necessary to bring them with you and show them to your audience; though one may use a sheet of paper in reading aloud an imaginary letter. Generally, to imitate with actual objects some substitute for the thing referred to only confuses your hearers. For private practice, however, the real objects should be handled, and then the same motions repeated without them, as this accustoms your hands and arms to their shape and size. To hold the hand three feet above the platform every time one mentions a child, is a muscular platitude; and a platitude is always an insult to an audience. Let your acting be rare, rather than overdone.

Dramatic art at its best will not be over-explicit, or leave nothing for the audience to guess; nor will it be too vague, laying everything on them.

Acting, more than anything else, must be sincere. "Art, seen through, is execrable." There has perhaps never been a period in the world's history when sham has been so hated as it is today. It excites open mirth. An ambitious minister, having seen Whitefield when silenced by a thunder storm kneel on the platform, saying with deep devotion: "God is speaking; let man be silent and listen to His voice," was so impressed by the effect produced upon the audience, that he determined to repeat it. When a thunder storm arose during his service, he fell upon his knees; and, peeking through his fingers to note the effect on his audience found them laughing. The act without the spirit is dead. Sincere dramatic action, if quite spontaneous, is profoundly impressive. In the middle of the past century, when Father Taylor pictured to his audience of sailors the descent of a sinner into hell, it brought those honest tars to their feet in a horror of suspense. A century earlier, the great Jonathan Edwards so likened the reprobate's position to a spider web stretched across a chimney's top, that his hearers grasped the seats in front of them lest they drop into the flames. Pictures of a burning hell would have no such effect today, in a modern theology, but the doom of a misspent life will never lose its terror for an intelligent congregation. Chesterfield, the most elegant man in England, was present when Whitefield, whose eloquent acting was the envy of even Garrick himself, described the sinner as a blind man, led by his dog, and feeling his way by his cane toward a precipice. As the hush of the scene fell and deepened, Chesterfield sprang to his feet, shouting: "O God, he's gone!"

A third form of dramatic art, equally effective, within its limits, is facial expression. A stolid face speaks an indifferent heart. Facial expression demands good light, and not too large an auditorium. It is perhaps unnecessary to warn you to beware of mannerisms, such as the Roosevelt squint, which in his case was the result of his poor eyesight; or contortions such as mark eccentric personalities; or the inexcusable habit of shutting the eyes, a habit induced by fear of the audience, and an effort to shut out the faces in front of you. What a speaker is saying is lost, when the mind of the audience is taken up by wondering whether "it hurts" or not. Xanthes:

"The eyes are the most expressive feature of the face. The orator should pay special attention to their expression. They will express surprise, fear, indifference, or shame, according as they are wide open,

half-closed, or lowered. The mouth opens in emotion, caused by fear
or sudden surprise. In grief, the corners of the mouth droop. The
lower lip extended forward indicates scorn, and sometimes ignorance.
The movement of the head thrown back, accompanied by an elevation
of the eyebrows, indicates audacity."

The face graphically expresses emotions and ideas. Copy the
deaf man's language for "sickness," and note the part his face
plays. When the lecturer on marriage warns young women not
to marry either ugly or silly men, he gives wise advice. But how
much more impressive he can be if he puts it with both face and
words.

Let your eyes follow gestures of direction: as when the hands
are lifted and folded in prayer; or as when you say, "over there."
The place for your eyes, when not glancing at your notes, or
following gestures of direction, is looking into the faces of your
hearers. An eighteenth century writer:

"The eyes are not to be *rolled* along the ceiling, as if the speaker
thought himself in duty bound to take care how the flies behave themselves. Nor are they to be constantly cast *down* upon the ground, as
if he were before his judge receiving sentence of death. Nor to be
fixed upon *one point*, as if he saw a ghost."

Don't look at the floor with your head cocked on one side, like
a robin. The gaze of your audience has nothing but friendli-
ness in it: they look at you in order to get what you are saying.
If you lose one of those valuable eyes, keep looking at its owner
until he returns it to you. For it can be of no use to him unless
you borrow it.

Remember that you cannot make your audience see what you
have not first seen yourself. Action of all sorts requires a keen
imagination. Imagination may be cultivated. Because a thing
is not seen, it need not therefore be unseeable. All friendship
depends to a large extent on the imagination, even the friendship
of God.

It is highly desirable that the speaker imagine as vividly as
he can, while he is speaking, any scenes or events he seeks to describe. Shall the speaker, asks Quintillian, make his audience
"see" the murderer striking down his prey unless the speaker
also "sees" in his imagination the very scene as he describes it?
A detailed discussion of this important matter will be found in

one of the volumes listed in the Bibliography, Kirkpatrick's *Creative Delivery*, etc. In some subtle manner, the audience will visualize clearly only what the speaker himself clearly imagines as he describes it. This is an art which requires practice, but which contributes significantly to the hold which the orator can gain over his material and his listeners.

19

THE CROWNING GIFT

The crowning gift of the speaker in public is summed up in a phrase of three words: *Earnestness of purpose.* In every profession, on every occasion, success hangs on earnestness of purpose. It includes the two transcendent elements of platform power: the one, earnestness, involving the whole personality of the speaker; the other, purpose, summing up all the qualities of eloquence.

The most important thing that the student will read in any book, or hear in any course of lectures, on speaking in public, is this: that the success of a speech depends on the purpose with which it is delivered. "We shall speak to no purpose, unless we have a purpose in speaking." The first question that you are to ask yourself is not, "What shall I speak on?" but "Why shall I speak?" When you reach the second stage of preparation, the main body of your speech, you are to ask yourself: "What end have I in view?" When you arrive at the third stage, that is, as you mount the platform, you ask yourself: "What am I here for?" That question, from the selection of your theme to the last sentence of your conclusion, is to remain uppermost in your mind. The purpose is the measure of success. That is my chief word to my students. For that reason I have placed this chapter at the end as the climacteric of the course. It is the key that unlocks the gates of power. To keep it in mind is to triumph with an audience, to grow into a place of strength, to forestall self-condemnation, self-condemnation which is the bitterest drop in failure's cup. As the direction of the weather vane is determined by the wind, so the object determines the subject.

Your purpose must be definite. The man that is a victim of

wandering desires gets nowhere. Psychology tells us that if you stumble while going upstairs, it is because you have not fully made up your mind that you want to go upstairs. A thrifty father does not depend on chance for the support of his family. He directs his business with an income in view. Burns:

> "To win Dame Fortune's golden smile,
> Assiduous wait upon her;
> And gather gear by every wile
> That's justified by honor."

Yet many a speaker "steps on the gas" with no definite idea of where he is going. "A fanatic," wrote Santayana, "is one who redoubles his effort after he has lost sight of his goal." Do you wonder that he feels uncertain as to the attitude his audience will take towards him? The cure for stage fright is to have fixed and vivid purpose in view.

There are many purposes that have ruled and are ruling public speakers. Lift the lid from your heart and examine carefully the ruling purposes of your life. Make sure that you are sincere in this. Dickens wrote in *Little Dorrit:* "Only the wisdom that holds the clue to all hearts and all mysteries can surely know to what extent a man can impose upon himself." An orator may discover that he has been finding it more blessed to receive than to give; that reputation weighs heavier than service; that money talks so loud that he cannot hear the cry of need; that applause is dearer than useful labor. A minister of the gospel may be seeking culture rather than Christ: he may be more eager to excel in a knowledge of the arts than in the art of winning a forgetful world for its Saviour. He may know the face of Christ better on canvas than in personal devotion. We speakers are often more ashamed of our errors in grammar than of our coldness of heart. We are careful of our appearance on the platform, but alas! for the nakedness of our souls! What shall we say of our self-satisfaction in service scamped, in opportunity seen dimly through half-blinded eyes? Every speaker has some purpose in view. What is it?

It may be to fill an engagement; and perhaps to get practice. Both of these are essential to success. Just as they are in the case of a physician. "The hour has come," the speaker says; "I am here; I will make my speech when I am called up." Then he goes to his next duty with the high sense of having fulfilled his obligation. But he does not raise the level of the day's routine.

A common purpose with speakers is the aim to make a first class speech. "Most speeches," they say, "are comparative failures; mine shall be a conspicuous success." With this end ever in view, he determines he will remember all the rules he has so carefully learned. "Previous preparation shall be attended to. I will come to the platform in fine physical condition. I will devote earnest and patient thought to my theme and analysis. My address shall be characterized by both unity and progress. It shall contain interesting illustrations, and sparkle with epigrammatic quotations. The expression shall be daylight-clear, and the delivery direct. I will dress suitably. The ventilation shall not be overlooked. I will avoid mannerisms, and the 'holy tone.' I will employ good diction. I will have the spirit of abandon. I will display the necessary force. I will use voice-modulation, pauses, inflections, restrained and fitting gesticulation," etc., etc. Ambition burns in your heart. You resolve: "This speech will be an event, an event long to be remembered by those that listen to it. I shall impress them by my wisdom and cleverness. I shall eclipse the other speakers on the program." This sort of thing is fatal, fatal. Beveridge: "Never try to be eloquent."

A third and worthier motive that may move a speaker is the wish to satisfy expectations. The committee that have invited him have had certain ends in view. The political party for whom he speaks wants their platform or their candidate advantageously presented. And there are the views of the majority of the audience to be taken into account. The desires of others must not be disappointed. Every speaker is in a position like that of a congressman who is expected to represent the views and wishes of his constituency. He naturally wants to please his audience. The wishes of one audience differ in toto from those of another; and this requires adjustment on his part, if he meets their demands. He must so speak as to satisfy on occasion Socialists, Fundamentalists, Modernists, a Lodge, the G.A.R., and to please his wife or sweetheart. This is the situation presented to a hard-headed Micaiah, II Chron. 18.12: "The messenger that went to call Micaiah spake to him, saying, Behold, the words of the prophets declare good to the king with one mouth: let thy word therefore I pray thee, be like one of theirs, and speak thou good." Such advice a voice whispers to every public speaker. Sometimes it is a leading individual whom he is expected to satisfy. Sometimes the gallery seem to be saying: "I hope he'll wade into that audience," thus creating one sentiment for the ground floor and the opposite sentiment for the gallery. So, he that makes it his chief aim to please his audience finds himself in straits.

There is but one effective purpose, and that is to do what needs to be done with your audience. Ulterior motives are inferior motives. Other aims than the sole one of what needs to be done with and for your audience, instead of being aids to the end in view, if placed first, become actual hindrances to your task. Admiral Dewey, steaming forth in Manila Bay with the explicit instructions of his government: "Find and destroy the Spanish fleet," observed a German battleship manoeuvring near the scene, and signaled: "Don't get between my guns and the enemy." Singleness of purpose brought him victory. The eternal choice of every speaker is between making a great speech and achieving a great result. He may do neither, but it is certain that he will never accomplish the former unless he aims at the latter. Shall I better my reputation, or shall I better the audience? Better your audience, and you will better both. The public takes no interest in the carpenter that takes more interest in his wages than in his employers. The author that seeks fame rather than the public weal misses both. It is that sort of thing that made the Boston writer, W. B. Hale, say with disgust: "There is nothing so extremely vulgar as success." Every move in life hangs on its purpose. Shall we go sailing, or shall we arrive at port? Count Lyof Tolstoy, sitting cobbling shoes in his basement workroom, looks out of the window as the boots go by: "There is a patch I put on that will keep its wearer warm! There are a pair of shoes that neither ice nor damp can penetrate!" Thus thinking of the protection and comfort he had provided, drudgery became a joy. His novels, essays, and doctrinal works, having the same ideal in view as his cobbling of shoes, made him the greatest man of his generation, as well as the most famous novelist of the age. So, as you reflect on your last speech,

ask yourself: "What did I do it for?" Speak not for effect, but
for effectiveness. Make it the aim of your life not to do well,
but to do good. Seek not expression, but impression. Joseph
Parker, to the clergyman seeking a charge who preached a sample
sermon to him: "Now I know why you have no parish: you have
been preaching to get that sermon off your mind, not into mine."
The minister whose aim is to serve his hearers to the utmost of
his strength and ability, speaks with authority. Whitefield, on
a sultry summer afternoon in the country, finding his audience
drowsy—a sight new to him—suddenly halts: "If I were here
talking to you in my own name you might go off to sleep; and
now and then rousing, ask: 'What does the babbler talk of?' but
I speak to you in the name of the Lord God of Hosts; and I must
and will be heard!" If there was the shame of failure in that
service, it was not in the pulpit.

This central purpose will never vary in its character, but it
may vary widely in its direction. When Webster pleaded the famous Dartmouth College case, his audience were stirred to tears.
Justice Story, who was present: "For the first hour we listened
to him with perfect astonishment, for the second with perfect
delight, for the third hour with perfect conviction." Your purpose may take one of three directions: (a) It may take the direction of instruction. Your purpose, in that case, being to teach,
you will employ clearness, succinctness, accuracy; i.e., some quality of mind. Or (b) your purpose may be inspiration, wishing
to bring enthusiasm, comfort, joy, or devotion; i.e., some quality
of soul. (c) It may be an appeal to the will, your purpose being
to lead your hearers to definite decisions. The ancients defined
eloquence as "the power to persuade." Wendell Phillips: "The
chief thing I aim at is the mastery of my subject. Then I try to
get my audience to think as I do." It was a saying among Cicero's
contemporaries that when they heard him speak they exclaimed:
"What matchless oratory! What perfection of argument the
ancient Greeks had! What faultless beauty of diction!" But when
they listened to Demosthenes, they cried: "Let us go and fight
Philip!" To illustrate the varied directions that one's purpose may take, suppose the subject to be *Culture*. If your purpose be to instruct, the treatment will deal with the impartation
of culture; if your purpose be inspiration, you will deal with

the thrill of the enjoyment of the beautiful; if your purpose be to rouse the will, you will stir the resolve for self-development. While some rhetoricians regard argumentation and persuasion as identical, in reality argumentation is turned into persuasion by the purpose of the speaker. You argue in order to persuade.

If the speaker is to become an outstanding platform force, it is not sufficient for him to have a purpose in speaking. He must have also earnestness, earnestness of purpose. "The emotions of the hearer depend on those of the orator." How few one hears that seem to care enough about their subject to make any one else care! Can any reader of these lines recall more than two or three speakers in his lifetime that have stirred him to the depths? I heard a man that had been in the ministry forty years say that he had never had but two singers in his choirs that put heart enough into their singing for him to call upon them for a solo following his sermon, though many of them had asked him to use them at that hour. He said he had known four in his con-gregations during those forty years, congregations that numbered thousands, who could pray in such a spirit as to stir the audience. Nearly all ministers and lawyers utter their pleas in a professional matter-of-fact manner that leaves their subject where they found it, many of them actually creating, by their way of presentation, a prejudice against their cause. A half-hearted speaker is a menace to the truth he would defend. He is a mirage, an *ignis fatuus*. *The Spectator,* No. 147: "We can talk of life and death in cold blood, and keep our temper in a discourse which turns upon everything that is dear to us." Such men's auditors are often more in earnest than they are themselves. They see the boat beached on the sand, and long for some mighty wave to lift and carry it out to sea on a useful mission. Dullness of heart is the chief cause of the speaker's failure on the platform, an in-difference to every one in the house except himself.

Earnestness is the one factor common to all great speakers. It gives them supremacy over their contemporaries. How dif-ferent from one another in native gifts are the foremost masters of the platform! Demosthenes the patriot, Paul the theologian, Marcus Aurelius the ethicist, Garrick the actor, Socrates the reasoner, Savonarola the reformer, Rutherford the affectionate, Voltaire the intellectual, Webster the oratorical, Beecher the sympathetic, Wendell Phillips the inspirational, Jowett the mystical, each is so different from the others that they would form data for a psychological study in oral expression. Yet in one sole respect they are alike, and that is in their earnestness of purpose. A half-dozen pieces of different-colored glass, placed in the fire, become the same color, each white hot. So Schiller, in *The Song of the Bell:*

> "It is in fiery motion
> That all forces come to light."

Natural gifts and education are aids to earnestness, though neither is essential to it, nor a substitute for it. All kinds of weapons are pointed in this glowing fire. Every natural endowment is fuel to the fire of an earnest purpose. Such purpose is the source of action. "Fire and fuel must get together!" cried McDowell.

That earnestness is the chief source of platform popularity, and of personal magnetism, is common testimony. Even without exceptional talent, or wit, or grace of person, have the men of flame won when their superiors failed. President Wilson: "Where there is a fire, thither will men carry their lamps to be lighted." Amazingly an audience responds to an earnest speaker: now cheers, now tears. Shurter: "Deliver your talk with all the strength, feeling, and approval that you would put into a struggle for your life."

Those that are afraid to let go the fires in their souls would better be afraid of the contempt felt by an audience for indifference. Though scientists claim to be able to produce light without heat, the discovery has not been applied to public speech.

When comes this culminating gift? How may earnestness of purpose be acquired? Maeterlinck: "The essential mission . . . is to live with all the ardor of which one is capable, as if his life were more important than any other to the destinies of humanity." Earnestness of purpose involves a conviction of the importance of the subject. Don't work for it: do not assume it; it does not come that way. It rises like the mist from soil that has lain under the sun. It is not manufactured; it grows, by reflection. Look over the faces of your expectant audience, and ask yourself: "What will happen, if they don't get it?" Earnestness involves a passion to make your subject known. Joan of Arc's name will be remembered with reverence while the race lasts. That peasant girl's earnestness set two nations on fire. Palissy, in quest of success: "Give me only fire enough, and these colors shall be burned into this china!" Flame makes fame.

Earnestness involves a strong sympathetic interest on your part in your hearer. "The way to have earnestness is to build it into the life." Men do not gather grapes of weeds. Earnestness of speech is kindled by conviction and fanned by affection.

Earnestness of purpose may be deepened by a sense of the shortness of the time. I have but one life: let that count. Over Ruskin's desk was a chalcedony slab bearing a single word:

TODAY

Dr. Samuel Johnson wore cut into his watchcase: "*Ἡ Νὺξ Ἔρχεται*" ("The night cometh"). Whatever your occupation, in which public speech is called for, it is the purpose that spells success.

> " 'Tis not for man to trifle:
>   Life is brief, and sin is here;
>   Our age is but the falling of a leaf,
>   A dropping tear.
>   We have no time to sport away the hours:
>   All must be earnest in a world like ours."

Speakers do not *suffer* enough. The world asked of Him who was its greatest citizen:

> " 'Lord, whence are those blood-drops all the way.
>   That mark out the mountain's track?'
>   'They were shed for one that had gone astray
>   Ere the Shepherd could bring him back;
>   And although the road be rough and steep,
>   I go to the desert to find my sheep.'
>   'Lord, Thou has here Thy ninety and nine,
>   Are they not enough for Thee?'
>   But the Shepherd made answer: ' 'Tis of mine
>   Has wandered away from me.'
>   Then up from the mountains, thunder-riven,
>   And up from the rocky steep,
>   There rose a glad cry to the gate of heaven:
>   'Rejoice, I have found my sheep!'
>   And the angels echoed, around the throne:
>   'Rejoice, for the Lord brings back his own!' "

QUESTIONS

Chapter I

Why is speaking in public "the most difficult of all arts"?
What four advantages has public speaking over the press?
How answer the charge that "talk is cheap"?
Is public speaking receiving more emphasis today than heretofore? Give some proofs.
Why are set rules not to be emphasized?
What is the nature of the relation between the speaker and his audience?
Give seven reasons for speaking well.
In what professions or trades is there absolutely no need for speaking well?
In what professions and trades is speaking well an asset?

Chapter II

Compare the speaking and administrative gifts.
How does public speaking differ from elocution?
How does the preacher's speaking compare with that of others?
Why is preaching difficult?
Why is the notion false that study makes one artificial?
What human needs call to the speaker?
Why should the speaker practice long and hard in private?
Should the speaker take a list of rules along with him to the platform? Why or why not?
Can the speaker forget all about the "how" of his speaking as he talks? Why or why not?

Chapter III

How may one become a successful speaker?
Name three reasons for thorough preparation.
What should be your feeling towards your audience?
Can the speaker deceive his audience?
Have imitations of others proved successful? How, and how not?
Name seven ways of self-preparation.
What do true manhood and womanhood include?
How become a conversationalist?
What two kinds of reading are recommended, and what is the benefit of each?
How acquire æsthetic refinement?
Name five rules for maintaining health.
What uses can conversation with his people have for the minister?

CHAPTER IV

Discuss the dangers of being over-concerned about a speech before its delivery.
Why wait a moment before beginning?
How feel towards your audience? How act toward them?
How is public speech like, and how unlike, conversation?
Discuss the use of the eyes, in relation to your audience.
Discuss your attitude toward your introduction.
What about making apologies?
If stalled, what next?
What spirit will win? Why?
Sum up briefly the seven aspects of the speaker's relation to his audience.

CHAPTER V

What is the importance of the material setting to a speech?
If outdoors?
Discuss the effect of poor ventilation on the audience. On the speaker.
Some ventilation devices?
What about lighting?
Heating?
Seating?
How meet distractions: from sexton? animals? babies? misbehavior?
Discuss ushers, their duties, and the speaker's relation to them.
How may distractions be turned to advantage by the alert speaker?
What type of church architecture would you favor? Why?

CHAPTER VI

What is the importance of the audience to the speaker?
Is knowledge of men enough for a speaker? Why or why not?
His temptations, with relation to his audience?
What is meant by "emotional centers" in an audience?
What kinds of hearers? How shall a speech be made, to suit them?
How is an audience the "echo" of the speaker?
How may audiences differ from each other? What does this mean for the
    speaker?

CHAPTER VII

What is the value of a good voice? Effects?
Importance of right use?
Helps to betterment?
Treatment for sore throat?
How begin? Why?
Tone for beginning? Advantages? Carrying tone? Effect of "throaty" tone?
What does it mean to know that "your voice is best for you"?
Why is having something to say and wanting to say it important in relation
    to voice?
Discuss the five aspects of voice improvement.

CHAPTER VIII

Why is it vital to vary the voice?
What is meant by varying the pitch?
How loud should one speak? Why?
How read the Bible? Poetry?
Why speak slowly?
Should a speech have a fixed rate? Why?
Name eight kinds of voice-quality.
What are imitative tones?
Tell how to find your optimum speaking pitch. Do you use it?
Why should the speaker avoid vocal monotony?
What is the value of the pause?

CHAPTER IX

How does the "holy tone" differ from the "adaption of voice to the idea"?
What is its effect on apparent length of address?
What things contribute to the feeling of solemnity on a preacher's part?
Name the objections to the "holy tone."
Is there more than one such "tone"? Name a few.
Cause? In the old? The young?
Cure?
What special opportunities does the minister have for speaking practice?

CHAPTER X

Can a speaker know when his speech is to be a success?
Where do success or failure chiefly rest?
Is he usually conscious of his mannerisms?
Three chief causes for them?
How get rid of them?
What is the best platform manner?
Four or five ways to acquire it?
What is "abandon"?
What is meant by "adapting the manner to the thought"?
Which manner to be shunned?

CHAPTER XI

What is platform magnetism?
What is it independent of?
Name prominent leaders who possess it.
Compare with the magnetism of electricity.
Where did the word *magnet* come from?
The first source of it?
Relation of health?
Second element?
How general is its appreciation?

Should it be often used on the platform?
Third element?
What is meant by "magnetic memory"?
Fourth and most important element?
Can magnetism be acquired? How soon?

Chapter XII

Name three reasons for saying a thing well.
How many words are used by the average person? Milton? Shakespeare?
What kinds of words are most effective?
Name words distinguished by nice shades of meaning.
How may a style achieve strength?
How enlarge your vocabulary?
Name four or five common errors in enunciation.
A rule for the habit of correct pronunciation?

Chapter XIII

What determines the choice of a subject?
Value of a two to five years' course?
Whence are themes found?
Name five styles of sermonizing.
Order of arrangement of a speech?
What should an introduction include?
Discuss three or four varieties of conclusion.
Name some characteristics of the topic or title.

Chapter XIV

At what point in the preparation of a speech should illustrations be chosen?
Their importance?
Their character?
How tell an anecdote? (Answer in detail.)
Best method of storing for instant use?
How index quotations from literature?
Name some of the sources of illustrations. Which are better, and which are poorer?
Discuss the risks involved in the use of illustration.

Chapter XV

Why only one idea in a speech? What kind of an idea?
What goes with unity?
Name four essential kinds of progress. How are these secured?
What is meant by progress in thought?
How do the several divisions further this?
Name the four things that constitute progress in delivery.
What kinds of addresses need not be brief?

Why do speakers talk too long? Cure?
Which is the more difficult to prepare, long or short talks?
How end gracefully?
Quote the sentence of J. M. Buckley.

Chapter XVI

Advantages of writing? Disadvantages?
Occasions for reading in full?
Advantages of memoriter speaking? Disadvantages?
Meaning of "extempore" speaking?
How avoid speaking without preparation?
Advantage of one page of notes? How written?
Six advantages of using no notes? Disadvantages?
Name four ways in which speeches may be prepared and delivered.

Chapter XVII

Essentials of an after-dinner speech?
What to do, if you are toastmaster?
In what respects does the lecture differ from an ordinary speech?
Necessary steps on the lecturer's part?
Name ten topics to be incorporated in the successful lecture.
How long preparation?

Chapter XVIII

The two main types of gesture?
Importance of dramatic action? How different from gesture?
Does the gesture accompany, precede, or follow the thought? Why?
What gestures should the eyes follow?
What one quality alone makes gestures "bad"?
Discuss the importance of sincerity in gesture and manner.
Discuss the value of vividly imagining the scenes one seeks to portray in his
    speaking.

Chapter XIX

What is the speaker's crowning gift?
On what one mental faculty does the success or failure of every speech depend?
Name three common purposes of speakers. The true one.
In what three directions may a purpose legitimately run?
What is the one common factor of all great speakers?
In what three ways may earnestness be acquired?

Which of these lectures have you needed most? Why?

BIBLIOGRAPHY

(The titles listed are but illustrative of a wide field of reading.)

General Speech

History

Platz, M. *The History of Public Speaking.* N.Y., 1935.
Sears, L. *The History of Oratory.* Chicago, 1896.

Theory and Study

Baird, A. C. *Essentials of General Speech.* N.Y., 1952.
Borden, R. C. *Public Speaking as Listeners Like It.* N.Y., 1935.

Brigance, W. N. *Speech Composition.* N.Y., 1953.
Briggs, L. M. *The Master Guide for Speakers.* Minneapolis, 1956.

Bryant, D. C. *Fundamentals of Public Speaking.* N.Y., 1947.
Carnegie, D. *Public Speaking.* N.Y., 1935.

Corson, H. *The Voice and Spiritual Education.* N.Y., 1908.
Crocker, L. *Public Speaking for College Students.* N.Y., 1954.

Dixon, J. *How to Speak.* N.Y., 1949.
Hegarty, E. J. *How to Write a Speech.* N.Y., 1951.

Higgins, H. N. *Influencing Behavior Through Speech.* Boston, 1930.
Mathews, B. *Notes on Speech-making.* N.Y., 1901.

Murray, E. *The Speech Personality.* Chicago, 1944.
Sarett, L. R. *Basic Principles of Speech.* Boston, 1946.

Winans, J. A. *Speech Making.* N.Y., 1938.
Woolbert, C. H. *Fundamentals of Speech.* N.Y., 1927.

Preaching

History

Dargan, E. C. *A History of Preaching.* Grand Rapids, 1954.
Jones, E. DeW. *The Royalty of the Pulpit.* N.Y., 1951.
Ker, J. *Lectures on the History of Preaching.* London, 1888.

Theory and Study

Baxter, B. B. *The Heart of the Yale Lectures.* N.Y., 1947.
Lyman Beecher Lectures on Preaching — Any of the long series.

Bowie, W. R. *Preaching.* Nashville, 1954.
Broadus, J. A. *A Treatise on the Preparation and Delivery of Sermons.* London, 1898.

Brown, C. R. *The Art of Preaching.* N.Y., 1922.
Kennedy, G. H. *Who Speaks for God?* Nashville, 1954.

Kirkpatrick, Robert W. *The Creative Delivery of Sermons.* N.Y., 1944.
Lee, M. W. *So You want to Speak?* Grand Rapids, 1951.

McClorey, J. A. *The Making of a Pulpit Orator.* N.Y., 1934.
Philips, F. *Manual of Elocution for the Minister.* Edinburgh, 1940.

Sharp, J. K. *Next Sunday's Sermon.* Phila., 1940.
Stewart, J. S. *Heralds of God.* N.Y., 1946.

Classical Rhetoric

Aristotle. *Rhetoric.* Cambridge, 1909. (Many editions.)
Blair, Hugh. *Lectures on Rhetoric.* London, 1803–06.

Cicero. *The Orator. Brutus.* Cambridge, 1939. (Many editions.)
Quintillian. *Institutes of Oratory.* London, 1921–22.

Thonssen, L. *Selected Readings in Rhetoric.* N.Y., 1942.
Whately, R. *Elements of Rhetoric.* N.Y., 1871.

Voice and Diction

Anderson, V. *Training the Speaking Voice.* N.Y., 1942.
Craig, W. C. *The Preacher's Voice.* Columbus, 1945.
Funk, W. *30 Days to a More Powerful Vocabulary.* Pocket Books.
Harper, R. M. *The Voice Governor.* Boston, 1940.

Karr, H. M. *Develop Your Speaking Voice.* N.Y., 1953.
Parkhurst, C. C. *Using Words Effectively.* N.Y., 1948.

Illustrations

Bryan, D. C. *The Art of Illustrating Sermons.* Nashville, 1938.
Crocker, L. *Henry Ward Beecher's Art of Preaching.* Chicago, 1934.

Prochnow, H. V. *The Public Speaker's Treasure Chest.* N.Y., 1942.
Sangster, W. E. *The Craft of Sermon Illustration.* London, 1950.

Interpretation

Woolbert, C. H. *The Art of Interpretative Speech.* N.Y., 1947.